THE
Most Beautiful Gardens
IN THE WORLD

To my nephews and nieces

ALAIN LE TOQUIN

THE
Most Beautiful Gardens
IN THE WORLD

Introduction by Michel Baridon
Text by Jacques Bosser

Translated from the French by Clare Palmieri

HARRY N. ABRAMS, INC., PUBLISHERS

"The passing cloud, the cool breeze,
the seed that drifts through the air, a sudden gust of wind,
the light that dims and brightens again—
so many things
imperceptible to unaccustomed eyes
transform the color and disturb the surface of the water."

—Claude Monet

The water lilies in Claude Monet's Impressionist garden at Giverny

Introduction

The garden is one of the most ancient of man's creations. The Bible presents it as the cradle of humanity, and in most religions a garden is an important part of the story of Creation. Because of their history, gardens deserve a place of honor in our cultural pantheon, but they have no such pretensions. A backyard brightened by a few daisies or a modest vegetable patch is as much a true garden as an intricate formal design that graces the landscape surrounding a palace. A veritable Proteus, the garden surprises us with its perpetual metamorphoses, and yet it steadfastly maintains its traditional role, which is to invite us to experience nature and to bid us enter for the pure pleasure of being in its company.

Let us understand clearly what we mean by simple things. One can be simple when one lives close to nature; the farmer's vegetable garden, a lovely salad, a perfect dahlia have their place, and this is as it should be. But the White Garden of Sissinghurst Castle, an entirely different affair, is also simple. Realizing that in the country a white flower takes one by surprise with its brilliant purity, its creator, Vita Sackville-West, intensified this effect by multiplying it within an enclosed space. Those who love the simplicity of nature in the wild will always appreciate this type of creation. The landscape gardener takes the flower for what it is but at the same time transcends it through their work as an artist. This difficult work is similar to that of the architect or the painter, but with different materials.

The Anglo-Japanese garden at the Château de Courances, France, was created between 1920 and 1930, next to the classical grounds designed by André Le Nôtre. The design was reworked in the twentieth century by Achille Duchêne.

Take painting and the decorative arts. In Pompeii, flower bouquets were painted under the porticoes that led to the garden; their fresh colors were preserved on the walls when Mount Vesuvius buried the city in the first century A.D. In the Middle Ages, fields of wildflowers pictured in tapestries spread a delicate lawn under the feet of lords and troubadours, and the ornate embroideries of the Renaissance and the Baroque era were decorated with colorful flowers and formal plantings reflecting the charm of Villandry, Versailles, and so many other gardens of the period. As landscape gardening spread throughout Europe, painting was honored above all the other arts. "Paint when you plant!" cried Alexander Pope, the most eloquent partisan of the new style. In fact, one has only to take a walk through Stourhead, in England, to see how much the importation of foreign flora, notably those from the Americas, has varied the palette of the landscaper. And what can one say of the great gardens of the last two centuries whose baskets of flowers and mixed borders, at the Bois des Moutiers, Apremont, and elsewhere, were so often inspired by the instructions of Chevreuil, the French chemist and color theorist who was also the scientific authority for the Impressionists, especially Claude Monet. And Monet, we must remember, never ceased shaping, planting, and decorating Giverny in order to paint it over a period of more than twenty years.

For a very long time, the work of designing gardens was given to architects. Even today in France the title of landscape architect (*architecte paysagiste*) is given to students who pursue a career in garden design, whereas in England the preferred term is *landscape gardener*. This discrepancy came about because of differences in the great traditions of the two countries, the former very attached to André Le Nôtre and his carefully structured gardens, and the latter to Lancelot ("Capability") Brown and the natural principles expressed by Alexander Pope. But even Brown and other landscapers of the eighteenth century shaped their gardens according to carefully drawn plans. Rejecting formal, geometric forms, the English landscapers dammed rivers to create ornamental lakes, opened up the woods to allow light, moved great rocks, set up waterfalls, and all this to represent nature as it actually is.

Nature—that is the word, the one that distinguishes the landscaper from the painter and the architect. The garden continually rebuilds itself with the passage of time. It lives under the infinite sky and claims kinship with the surrounding landscape; it gets along well only with those who know its soil, its orientation, its water sources, and the plants it favors. The garden asks these designers to look ahead to what it will become in a year, in two, ten, or twenty years. In exchange for so many demands, it offers to become a place like no other, a place where one is outdoors yet at home; a place of both solitude and company; a place that ceaselessly changes but always remains itself. In short, the garden is like us. To go into the garden is to enter into ourselves. Philippe de Dangeau recounted in his memoirs that Louis XIV used to take long walks around the Grand Trianon, even in severe cold or in fog, even when he was an old man. Jean-Jacques Rousseau, who was a very different individual, used to cross Ermenonville Park to meditate by the Desert de Retz. At Suzhou, in the deep valley of the Yangtze river—whether at Wangshi Yuan or at Zhuo Zheng Yuan, under the Ming dynasty or the Qing—the sage would make his way to a particular pavilion according to the hour of the day or the aspect of the moon in order to harmonize his thoughts and feelings with the appearance of the garden.

What is most striking with regard to the special relationship we have with gardens is our common ability to retain our identity through years of constant change. Thus we can walk directly into the past to rest from the long day. A garden will assume its place in the Italy of the Medicis, in the France of the Sun King, or in Imperial Rome. To experience these images is a great intellectual pleasure that gives substance to our memories of a voyage. For those who know their history, gardens read like an open book. At Stourhead the guides will tell us that the garden was created by Henry Hoare II, a banker from Bristol, and they will emphasize the many allusions to the *Aeneid* that one finds here and there among the statuary and in the little garden buildings. They may also add that the great landscape artist J. M. W. Turner painted several scenes at Stourhead, including the magnificent pantheon, whose white portico is reflected in the dark waters of the lake. If we knew a little more, we could add that the memory of Henry Hoare's son still inhabits these grounds. Young, brilliant, and cultivated, he carried the hopes of his family as Aeneas carried those of Rome, and he shared the enthusiasm of his father for the paintings of Claude Lorrain. He sailed to Italy in search of more works by the famous landscape painter but fell victim to an epidemic of plague and never returned. His inconsolable father borrowed the design of Stourhead's pantheon from Claude's painting *Landscape with Aeneas at Delos*, a work by a French painter they had both loved. The tragedy that struck this family still finds a sad echo in the great stillness of nature.

The history of gardens is far from simple, as the stories of Sanspareil and Schwetzingen demonstrate, but complexity adds much to the intellectual pleasure that the gardens provide. In Europe this history stems from two traditions that have their roots in classical antiquity. The first was the enclosed garden the Romans had cultivated, the *hortus*; the second and opposing style was the garden park, which was made fashionable by Roman generals returning from their campaigns in the East. In marrying these two traditions, Cicero, Pliny, and many others created an original art form that came to value the rural character of their estates while embellishing them with statues and plants that were cut and trimmed in a technique called *topiarius*, what we know today as topiary. The Romans accomplished all this while carefully creating the best views of the surrounding countryside from their villas and their porticoes. One finds these characteristics in marvelous balance in the Italian Renaissance gardens, such as those we see today at Castello Ruspoli and Villa Gamberaia, or at the French version, Ambleville.

Europeans were not the only ones to create gardens. Today, people who travel widely can experience gardens that owe little or nothing to Greece and Rome. China, Japan, and the Middle East developed their own cultural forms. However, the gardens of Islam are not as far removed from Greco-Roman culture as one might assume. The translations made by the caliphs of Baghdad in the ninth, tenth, and eleventh centuries familiarized the scholars of the era with Greek geometry and Roman agronomists. The strict forms of the Persian garden—the careful calculation of slopes to create the tinkling of running water, the aerial architecture that one sees in Granada, Spain, in northern India, in Persia, or in Bagh-e Fin, for example—all owe something to Euclid, Thales, and Vitruvius. One senses the familiar and feels at home in foreign lands.

To understand the gardens of China and Japan, on the other hand, one must adapt intellectually to their creation and their significance. You feel as if you are in a place both ancient and modern—ancient because geomancy plays a very important role and because one cannot feel the power of geometry, although that is, ironically, what makes Asian gardens seem modern to us. By imparting an awareness of a more thoughtful and sensitive approach to nature, and in teaching us the complexity of its systems, the ecology of the Far East compels us to consider nature in its own right, not as a material to be molded to our will by a bulldozer or an asphalt spreader. The new Land Art and its subtle constructions are close cousins to the art of the Far Eastern gardener, who might leave the tangled roots of an ancient tree to create their own wild path. Taking a walk through the gardens at Suzhou or Kyoto is enough to convince us that we have much to learn from this way of living with nature and letting nature speak for itself.

To recount the different traditions that have made the gardens of the world what they are today, and to highlight the most representative among them, is to take an armchair tour through the pages that follow in the capable hands of Alain Le Toquin and Jacques Bosser. We of the twenty-first century know well that the time for discovering great, unknown gardens belongs to the past, as when François Bernier, the envoy of Jean-Baptiste Colbert in India, marveled at the sight of the newly built Taj Mahal, or when Pierre Loti described the empress of Japan walking with her ladies-in-waiting at the edge of a pond that reflected "in long, soft streaks the violet and the orange; the blue and the yellow; and the green and the purple of their fairy costumes." We also know that the Far East can be reached in a single day by air, and that we have the means to capture and bring back home the images that in former times could be conveyed only by the writer's pen.

The essential images of a garden are those that reveal the spirit of the place and its meaning. These pictures are to gardens what portraits are to people: they capture the moment when they are most themselves, the moment they wish to prolong. People love to relive the beautiful moment or the feeling they have just discovered. "That strain again," says Orsino to the musicians in *Twelfth Night*.

Alain Le Toquin and Jacques Bosser also take us to gardens that are less well known because they are off the beaten path or because they have been created only recently. These include, of course, those of Iran, the stunning Titoki Point Garden of New Zealand, and the gardens of bald cypress in Moncks Corner, South Carolina. Here as well are represented two magnificent gardens of very recent vintage: Little Sparta and Portrack House, both in Scotland. Little Sparta is a manifesto of art in which sculpture and inscriptions radiate both humble and trenchant meanings in the mysterious woods and thickets of Pentland Hills. The other, Portrack House, is both a monument and a story cleverly composed by an architectural theorist who expresses the contemporary concepts of physics and genetics in the forms of nature.

This volume is a voyage into time, and a voyage around the planet. Let us go then to the gardens of the world.

—*Michel Baridon*

Pages 16–17: Sleeping nymph in the Sacred Wood of Bomarzo, not far from Rome, a sixteenth-century creation that defies classification

Pages 18–19: Designed about 1750, this boxwood labyrinth in the gardens of the Château de la Gaude, near Aix-en-Provence, France, represents one of the last masterpieces of the formal French style.

Pages 20–21: A recent creation of British inspiration, the gardens at Angélique in Normandy, France, offer visitors a feeling of intimacy.

Bagh-e Shahzdeh

The world's first parks were planted in the ancient Near East by Sumerian and Babylonian rulers, and these were prototypes for the Persian bagh, or garden, which provided a refuge from the torrid heat of the desert and a place for meditation or recreation. These gardens made use of the most sophisticated irrigation techniques, originally developed by the Babylonians and later perfected by the Persians. Although Bagh-e Shahzdeh is a relatively recent garden, it is one of the most dramatic illustrations of the victory of water over the desert.

Above: The gardens at Bagh-e Shahzdeh stretch out at the foot of the mountains southwest of Tehran.

Opposite: The earthen wall surrounding the gardens was restored in 1991.

In the history of human civilization, the garden is not a demonstration of man's dominance over nature, but an evocation of the creation of the world. The oldest surviving garden is the hunting park created by the king of Persia, Cyrus the Great (d. 529 B.C.) in his capital city of Pasargadae. The Greek soldier Xenophon, in a history of his military exploits in Persia written about 394 B.C., described this park, or *pairidaeza* (meaning "surrounded by walls"), as *paradeisos*, from which we derive the modern word "paradise." The dream of a protected place at the origin of the world, synonymous with the happiness that was lost, was a significant part of Zoroastrianism in Persia, and the idea of paradise remains a common element in the world's three great monotheistic religions today—Judaism, Christianity, and Islam. For millions of people, paradise is a beautiful garden.

The Persian garden was walled to protect it from inopportune visitors, thieves, and enemies and also to block the burning desert winds. The ground was divided into rectangles by narrow stone channels, or rills, that were laid crosswise radiating from the central pool. These rectangular divisions, which were periodically filled with water, marked the areas designated for the cultivation of flowers or trees, for pavilions or terraces, or for pools. This arrangement, taken up again by the Arab conquerors, became widespread throughout the Muslim world from Morocco to Spain to India.

Bagh-e Shahzdeh (The Prince's Garden) was created by Naser ad-Douleh in 1878, when he was governor of Kerman, an important city 500 miles southeast of Tehran. A great rectangle in green—the color of happiness in the Koran—the garden blooms in a desert land at the foot of a rugged chain of mountains. It served as the governor's summer retreat, a short interval of luxury, and no doubt of happiness as well. Ella Sykes, an English woman who visited the garden in 1905, spoke of the "water sprays rising into the air, which the August sun, sparkling through the haze, transforms into brilliant, showy rainbows." The presence of such stunning luxuriance in the midst of a blazing desert depends, of course, on a source of water—water that is harnessed in the mountains and travels for miles via an underground aqueduct to irrigate the gardens. The operating principle of this system is simple gravity, which explains the majestic fountain in cascading steps that forms the garden's focal point. Sixteen compartments converge on each of its sides, and these are planted in roses, immense trees, pear trees, and grenadines.

The architectural style is fairly eclectic. The walls and outbuildings were built with traditional terra-cotta vaults, while the elegant governor's pavilion features a curious modernity in an otherwise classical design. The entrance pavilion was designed in the Persian style of the nineteenth century—brick ornamented with gleaming blue ceramic tile. After the death of Naser ad-Douleh, Bagh-e Shahzdeh survived a long period of near neglect before being restored after the Islamic Revolution in 1979. Now a tourist site, the garden opens a page on a period of Iranian history that is little known in the West, that of the Qadjar dynasty. It also illustrates the dream of a governor who was perhaps restless and bored in this arid region and wanted to re-create the Garden of Paradise.

Following pages: The garden-oasis of Bagh-e Shahzdeh blooms within protective walls in a semi-desert region, evoking an image of the Garden of Eden.

Panorama: The chain of pools, whose fountains are fed by simple gravity, ends at the entrance pavilion.

Above: Lacquered bricks decorate the walls of the entrance pavilion in nineteenth-century Persian style.

Iran Bagh-e Fin

The Persian garden was not designed for strolling. The prince was carried in his sedan chair to an open pavilion or to the edge of a pool to meditate, hear music, write verse, or listen to recitations. There the air was cooler than in the desert; the gentle sound of the fountains, the slight rustle of branches in the breeze, and the scent of the roses and jasmine brought a dreamy joy to the senses.

Above: Iran's most ancient garden, Bagh-e Fin, was actually built in the eighth century but did not acquire its present form until the sixteenth. This is the reflecting pool in front of the bath house.

Opposite: Smaller pool in front of the bath house

Since the sixteenth century, poets, historians, and adventurers have praised the elegant refinement of Bagh-e Fin, one of the most famous gardens of ancient Iran, located 155 miles from Tehran on the road to Isfahan. The garden is thought to have been created about 1,200 years ago by Sassanian kings. A shah of the Safavid dynasty redesigned it about 1590, when it took the shape we know today, despite several important changes.

In the past, the garden was surrounded by desert, but now it can be found in a suburb of the city of Kashan, although the garden's high walls continue to protect it from prying eyes. To enter, one passes through a monumental entryway, which is topped with a cupola and four slender towers. At the center, opposite the entryway, is a vast pavilion, or *suffeh*. The six-and-a-half-acre enclosure is outlined by a canal that runs along the walls and is then divided into six sections by three perpendicular canals. Two of these intersect in the interior of the pavilion and supply a huge square pool built at one end. One of the charms of this particular garden is that the bottom of each canal is lined with turquoise earthenware tiles; the waters that flow over the tiles create luminous blue-green patterns under the foliage.

The pools are made of marble, and some are filled to overflowing. The supply of water from a local source is assured, thanks to the ingenious traditional system of *qana*, which collects water runoff from nearby mountains through a series of connected wells. Near the entryway stands an ancient bathhouse, which is famous for having been the scene of a prime minister's assassination in 1852. Other buildings were added in the nineteenth century.

Bagh-e Fin was once celebrated for the gentle sound of its waters and the intoxicating scents of its flowers, but the flowers are nearly gone. The gardeners have tried to re-create the flowerbeds, but the hundred-year-old eucalyptus, plantain, and fig trees now let in very little light. Restored and carefully maintained, the garden has been an inspiration for numerous travelers, including writer Vita Sackville-West, creator of the gardens at Sissinghurst Castle, who became interested in Bagh-e Fin during her trip to Iran in 1926. Bagh-e Fin is one of the last authentic examples of the art of Islamic gardening at its highest level.

A narrow canal that connects all the pools runs alongside the protective perimeter wall, a feature of ancient Persian garden design.

Little water jets arranged in the shape of a clock punctuate the main canal and the pools. The principle of gravity keeps them supplied with water.

The main canal is enhanced with a lining of turquoise lacquered tiles and dozens of fountains that constantly refresh the air.

Above: This pool in the lower hall in the central pavilion is formed by the intersection of two canals.

Opposite: The central pavilion, seen from the outside

Majorelle Garden

Marrakech •

MOROCCO

The concept of soul certainly applies to gardens. The spirit of a place, its history, or deep sentiments can contribute to the sense of soul, but it also incorporates the mystical notion that trees and flowers love to grow there. To create a garden, therefore, is to enable its soul to transcend being merely a piece of nature, a collection of plants, or a catalogue of species. The most interesting garden in Marrakech owes its creation to a painter, a fashion designer, and a skillful mediator.

Above: The square pool and the museum were recently refurbished by the Majorelle Trust.

Opposite: An intimate terrace behind the museum

Jacques Majorelle (1886–1962) was a fine painter, who, in the eyes of his critics, made the mistake of becoming a representational artist and being proud of that decision. Originally from the Lorraine, the son of cabinetmaker Louis Majorelle, Jacques arrived in Morocco in 1917 to treat his failing health. He spent his whole life there in a state of delight that is revealed in his art. His works are powerful, structured, determined, and somewhat ethnologic, and they captured the soul of a country that was still medieval on the eve of its modern transformation. In 1923 Majorelle had a huge house built for himself in Guélig, the European quarter of Marrakech. He decorated it with mosaics and woodwork that he painted in strong, contrasting colors. He then launched into the planting of an immense garden—nearly ten acres at one point—and this became his new passion.

In a few years, more than 1,800 varieties of cactus, tropical flowers, and ferns, and 400 varieties of palm transformed a patch of palm grove into a Garden of Eden. In 1931 Majorelle had a modern workshop built a short distance from the house because he and his wife had transformed the rear of the house into a modern center for arts and crafts using traditional artistic techniques. Majorelle presented his creations at the Paris International Exposition des Arts Décoratifs in 1925 and later produced the interior decoration for the famous Mamounia Hotel, one of whose guests, Winston Churchill, loved to visit his house. The size of the garden was reduced in 1955, and after his death, the property was neglected. After 1981, Yves Saint Laurent and Pierre Bergé bought it and returned the garden to the former 1930s splendor. They now belong to the Majorelle Trust.

The Majorelle Garden is more than a simple history of famous people and great talent. It is an original work. "Everything here bespeaks painting," said Bergé. "I often dream of these colors, which are unique," added Saint Laurent, who designed some of his collections there. This oasis is an astonishing production of a master colorist. Designed and painted by Majorelle, the intense cobalt blue that adorns every architectural element is the color against which all the others are compared: the brick-red floors, the chromium-yellow vases, the infinite shades of gray-green and yellow-green of the cacti, the emerald of the palms, the sheen of the water lilies, the blazing bougainvilleas, the subtle rose of the tamarisks, and the rich white of the jasmines. The water in the garden gently murmurs in pools surrounded by borders of the same blue, and from path to path the visitor finds himself taken by the magic of the scents—magnolias, eucalyptus, hawthorn, fig trees, and rosemary—and the smell of the earth warmed under the sun. A palette of colors, sounds, scents, and materials, Majorelle Garden is quite simply one of the painter's most beautiful works.

The water lily pool, bordered in the famous Majorelle blue

"I often dream of these colors, which are unique." —Yves Saint Laurent

The square pool with a few of the
garden's hundreds of different cacti

Panorama: Behind the garden stands the
museum, which is dedicated to
Moroccan folk art. The rear facade,
here, has recently been restored.

Above: The water lily pool

Nymphaeum of Villa Visconti Borromeo Litta

Water is an essential element in the Baroque garden—in pools, plant beds, canals, and fountains, and in the nymphaeum pavilions devoted to the water sprites of antiquity. At the immense Villa Visconti Borromeo Litta in Lainate, today located in the midst of a Milanese suburb, one can discover an extraordinary example of such a neoclassical pavilion.

Built in the seventeenth century and enlarged in the eighteenth, the luxurious Villa Visconti Borromeo Litta belonged first to the Visconti Borromeos and then by marriage to the Litta family, the wealthiest landowners in Italy. There the Litta family put on sumptuous parties, which were difficult to arrange in Milan because of the rebellious nature of the population.

It was during the Renaissance that nymphaeum pavilions first appeared, inspired by Homer and his description of Odysseus and the nymph Calypso in her grotto. These stone pavilions were built over a spring that supplied the fountains, pools, and sprays—water constructions that became ever more sophisticated. Accomplished artists were called upon to decorate these architectural fantasies, which offered welcome relief in the hot summers and an opportunity to entertain guests in luxury with an ingenious and artistic theme. The very complex nymphaeum of Lainate was built by Pirro I Visconti between 1585 and 1589, but its terra-cotta ornaments were replaced a century later with elements in more durable tufa stone. Beyond the entryway, which is lined with railings and basins containing jets of water, the pavilion has seven rooms—some made to look like a grotto—with water jets surging from the floors, statuary in fine Carrera marble, and preposterous frescoes that have maintained their vivid colors. For more than two centuries, all Europe has filed through this garden, marveling at the sight. After his visit, the writer Stendhal recalled, "As I placed my foot on the first step of a certain stairway, six jets of water surged around my legs."

At the end of the main corridor one comes upon *Venus Surprised at Her Toilet*, carved in Carrera marble by Francesco Carabelli in the eighteenth century.

The "ancient" grotto with a floor of marble mosaic, from which erupt very fine water jets that spray unsuspecting visitors. The walls are decorated with grotesques and naiads, or water nymphs, among which is *The Temptress*, shown at the center.

Right: One of the "sitting rooms" in the Nymphaeum, whose walls are decorated in the ciottoli technique, in which tiny pebbles are mixed with chips of marble, quartz, and even semiprecious stones and used to form designs like those seen on textiles or carpets

Following pages: The semicircular grotto, surrounded by stalactites and Carabelli's nymphs, fauns, and *Venus Surprised*, all veiled by the sprays of water.

Italy Castello Ruspoli

The castle of Vignanello is an enormous fortress that dominates the verdant landscape of northern Latium, the classic territory that includes Rome. The present-day villa has remained in the same family since the sixteenth century and now belongs to Princesses Claudia and Giada Ruspoli. Its ancient facade, with its unusual windows and Ghibelline crenellation, has been darkened by time, and its elevation belie the presence of its gardens—which remain in the purest Italian style.

Above: Having remained in the possession of one family for more than five centuries, this formal Renaissance garden is one of the most authentic and best preserved in Italy.

Opposite: During the evening, a small drawbridge separates the villa from the garden and the park.

For hundreds of years, the great Italian families who were related to the papacy had their country palaces in Latium. Located on a promontory, wedged into the volcanic lava, the castle of Vignanello was built on the ruins of an ancient Benedictine monastery. Pope Clement VII presented it as a gift to his niece Beatrice Farnese, whose daughter married into the Marescotti-Ruspoli family. The first step in the process of transforming the castle into a château, along with the commission to create a park, was taken on by Antonio da Sangallo the Younger (1485–1546). The Ruspoli family was so attached to this estate that they enlarged and embellished it until the end of the eighteenth century.

For the most part, the gardens are the work of the energetic Ottavia Orsini, who married the count of Vignanello in 1574. She was a lady of means, as her father was the designer of the famous Bosco Sacro di Bomarzo (Sacred Grove of Bomarzo; 1551). She modernized the château at the end of the sixteenth century and accomplished the great earth-moving work necessary for the installation of new gardens. The gardens were irrigated by distant water sources, and according to the inventory of 1658, the garden was composed of a *giardino di verdure*, or Garden of Greenery, a little Secret Garden, and a bit farther away, the parks called Barco and Barcetto. Virtually nothing has changed since that time.

The Garden of Greenery is the perfect example of the Italian garden. Its rectangular shape forms a balcony over a deep valley, and rows of clipped laurel, plum, and boxwood trees divide the garden into twelve sections, or compartments. At each corner there is a terra-cotta pot planted with an old rose in a pastel color. The interior of each section is occupied by sculpted bushes that show various motifs or the initials of Ottavia Orsini and those of her sons, Sforza Vinco and Galeazzo. At the very center of the whole composition, a single water jet rises from an exquisitely ornamented basin.

The Garden of Ruspoli represents an era in history when the art of topiary, which flourished in the Middle Ages and the Renaissance, reached its peak of development in Europe's fine gardens. The French carried it to great heights at Vaux-le-Vicomte and at Versailles. The Italian style, charming and intimate, either achieved magnificent splendor or fell into meaningless excess. Yet nowhere are the pleasure of perfumed roses and the scent of boxwood more intense than when the sun sets on the ancient garden of Ruspoli.

A large terra-cotta pot holding a lemon or rose tree softens the formal geometry of the garden's composition at the corner of each section.

Built as a fortress in the
Middle Ages, the austere
Castello Ruspoli was
transformed into a villa
between 1531 and 1538,
probably according to plans
by Antonio da Sangallo the
Younger, before it was
reworked in the seventeenth
and eighteenth centuries.

Below the Garden of
Greenery, at the upper left, is
the charming Secret Garden,
a balcony-in-the-sky above
the valley.

Italy Villa Gamberaia

ITALY

Settignano

"Sometimes, she told me, she would leave the house at dawn to swim in one of the pools in the water garden, or take a walk at night along the cypress alley." Thus wrote Bernard Berenson of Princess Catherine Jeanne Ghyka in his Memoirs. *She acquired the estate of Gamberaia in the late nineteenth century, and as she aged and her beauty faded, she cloistered herself there for the rest of her days.*

Above: View of the garden balcony over the Arno Valley. In the foreground is the water parterre installed by Princess Ghyka at the beginning of the twentieth century. The bowling green is at the left.

Opposite: The side entrance to the villa faces the great supporting wall of the upper terrace.

I s it a question of scale or one of humanity? Whichever it may be, the infinite charm of the gardens of Tuscany speaks as eloquently to people of the twenty-first century as it does to those of the sixteenth. The sky, earth, and water call upon all the senses to enable us to experience the clever enchantment of this place. The effects are elegant, but without the magnitude (or pretension) of the classic French style. Here in Italy, nature is confined rather than constructed, for that would be an impossible task for a sensible Italian, although not contrary to English thinking. The Tuscans have cultivated the art of the true garden, conceived for pure joy.

Before entering into the hands of Princess Ghyka, sister of Queen Natalia of Serbia, the estate of Gamberaia possessed a very long history, but one tranquil enough to have been forgotten and thus preserved. Although built in 1610 for Zanobi di Andrea Lapi, Gamberaia was the archetype of the Tuscan style of the late sixteenth century: simple, luminous, and functional, with rural roots that had not yet disappeared. The construction required large excavations and earth-moving, which made possible the creation of a vast garden, neatly outlined by walls and supplied with water from several sources, which explains the vibrant green of the lawns. The land on the hillside was organized around a green space for lawn bowling some 750 feet long, a kind of interior roadway around which were situated the villa, a string of outbuildings, a hanging garden of lemons, a rock garden, and the famous water garden, which at the time was little more than a fish pond. The bowling green was closed at one end by a nymphaeum pavilion, and the water garden terminated in a wall of cypress, sculpted in the form of archways that looked out onto the valley.

Verdant hedgerows, trees trimmed into spherical shapes, boxwood borders, and terra-cotta vases resting on pedestals create a geometric space that is both rigid and natural.

A simple description of its architecture cannot explain the miracle of Gamberaia. The gardens give the impression of having been transported to us intact, straight from their beginnings, when actually they represent several centuries of care and transformation. Following the Lapi family, the Capponis became the owners of Gamberaia in 1717, and they enlarged the gardens and created designs of sculpted boxwood. They also installed statuary, built the nymphaeum, and created the rock garden. "This open-air boudoir [is] more charming than one can imagine," wrote Harold Acton, the British historian and art critic. At the beginning of the twentieth century, we find Princess Ghyka calling upon two of the most celebrated Italian landscape designers of the era, Martino Porcinai and Luigi Messeri. They had the intelligence and sensitivity to respect the work that the centuries had produced in this extraordinary balcony of a garden overlooking the Arno Valley and the city of Florence.

Sophisticated and poetic, the gardens of Gamberaia were one of those private addresses known to the upper-class aesthetes who traveled around Italy at the beginning of the twentieth century, and their glowing descriptions soon made it an obligatory stopover. The closing days of World War II witnessed the pointless destruction of the villa, but it was reconstructed exactly as it had been in its rural splendor at the beginning of the seventeenth century. The present owners, the Zalum family, have taken up the task from all previous owners who have loved this place since 1610. All of them understand how to preserve the emotion that arises each time one take takes that little road between the rows of olive trees that leads to the villa and its hidden gardens.

The rock chamber with its stunning balustrades was carved into the terrace in the early thirteenth century.

A romantic view of the villa's gardens, which reach
toward Settignano on the hills overlooking Florence

Villa Lante

Italy

Jacopo Barozzi da Vignola was one of those remarkable Italians who could masterfully carve a statue, draw architectural plans for a palace, envision a great tomb, or design a garden. In the ancient region of Latium, at Lainate, he designed one of the most extraordinary gardens from the pivotal Mannerist period between the Renaissance and the Baroque era.

The gardens of the Villa Lante have attracted visitors from the time they were completed in the sixteenth century. The originality of the layout, the choice of statuary, the design of the pools, and the wonderful site—all of this has inspired wonderment. Many different elements were artfully combined in this Mannerist ensemble to produce a promenade of marvels and of cleverly engineered humor. The visitor encountered silly water surprises, obscure symbols, ancient iconography, and the latest wonders of hydraulic progress. Michel de Montaigne passed through the region in 1581 and wrote of his adventure and stupefaction at Villa Lante in his *Voyage en Italie.*

Cardinal Gambara received the estate from Pope St. Pius V as part of the archbishopric of Viterbo. He hastened to engage the architect of his prestigious relative, Alessandro Farnese, the duke of Parma and Piacenza, who had just finished the transformation of the fortress of Caprarola into a sumptuous villa just a few miles away.

The first sight of the villa from the little town of Bagnaia is surprising as this is not a villa in the usual sense of the term, but two symmetrical pavilions, one built in 1578, the other in 1612. From the park of the villa, one has the impression that the gardens are suspended over the city because one sees only the rooftops. These perceptions are most unlike those that strike the visitor to such prestigious edifices of the epoch as the Villa Giulia in Rome, Villa Caprarola, or Villa d'Este in Tivoli. But Villa Lante is a place of refined delights and a summer refuge, not a manifestation of power.

The Moorish Fountain is at the end of the water chain that divides the park, whose greenery looks down upon the villa and its gardens.

68

Panorama: Detail of the Fountain of the Giants, one of the most important Italian Mannerist fountains from the second half of the sixteenth century

Above: Detail of the Fountain of the Dolphins, a major element of the "theater of water" that distinguishes the gardens of the Villa Lante

The complex garden plan develops along a straight line punctuated by pools and fountains. From the top of the gardens down, a water chain (*catena d'aqua*), or a waterfall in steps like an aqueduct flowing downhill, creates fascinating eddies and optical illusions. It supplies first the Fountain of the Deluge, which is situated between two temples dedicated to the Muses, and then the Fountain of the Dolphins; below is the Fountain of the Giants (Tiber and Arno), followed by that of Pegasus, between the grottoes of Neptune and Venus. Finally, at the bottom, the water reaches the Moorish Fountain, where four Moors on a central islet lift up the coat of arms of the Gambara family.

Of the principal architectural elements, three inventions in the Mannerist style fascinate visitors: the water chain; the Cardinal's Table, a stone buffet table, twenty-two feet long, which contains a water trough in the center to cool wine, and other water elements; and the Water Organ, a tour-de-force of hydraulic engineering. The numerous water jets of this staggered fountain can be controlled by the leader of a small orchestra so that it flows in rhythm to the music.

Atop the hill, the gardens were set down in a park with pavilions, grottoes, and small structures, but in places nature takes over, blocking the view in spite of its system of paths and walkways.

Little has changed over the course of the centuries. The gardens of the villa have preserved the aesthetic and intellectual charms they possessed when they first opened. Guests must have loved to walk through this water wonderland, taking delight in the boxwood labyrinths or cool relief under the trees of the park that gave shelter from the suffocating heat of the Latium summers. Surrounded by walls and isolated from the city, the Villa Lante was an island of refinement and pleasant luxury in a time of political unrest. The ancient symbols were brought to the service of a dreamy aesthetic, and presented in a way that gave meaning to the period—between the Renaissance, which saw the emergence of the individual, and the Baroque, which would see him conquer the world.

The famous Cardinal's Table is equipped with a trough of cool water running down the middle. One can easily imagine the table laden with an exquisite feast, fine wines cooling in the trough, and sparkling chandeliers hanging overhead.

So remarkable was Vignola's idea of the water chain (*catena d'aqua*) that several neighboring villas copied it for their gardens.

France # Versailles

Versailles
FRANCE

Of all the creations presented in this compilation, Versailles is the only true archetype, that of the French garden. Its history, however, is not a simple one. Gardens of this type created elsewhere do not add up to Versailles, and the Versailles that we know today is not the one that Louis XIV loved to show his guests. Still, it remains one of the most famous gardens of the Western world.

Above: An entrance to the king's kitchen garden, begun in 1678 by Jean-Baptiste de La Quintinie near the Swiss Lake "for the king's walks and his pleasure"

Opposite: The kitchen garden comprises one huge square for vegetables and twenty-nine enclosed gardens for fruit trees. These are trees of the passe-crassane variety, a pear-quince hybrid.

People have long talked and written about the secret meanings in the design of the palace of Versailles and its grounds, about the role of the sun at its rising and setting, about the omnipresence of Apollo, and the dominance of nature, to the point of making the king a pagan god around which the world turned. However, aside from a youthful interest in court ballets featuring characters in golden armor, Louis XIV has always been presented as a Christian king more interested in the promotion of the French church than in the fantasies of Apollo. Seventeenth-century France was fascinated with symbols and allegories. From 1670 onward, the symbol of the sun disappeared from all décor, to be replaced by portraits of the king. At the same time, this absolute monarch took an avid interest in gardens and developed a faithful friendship with landscape architect André Le Nôtre (1613–1700). The king loved to take walks along the *allées*. Even during droughts, when the fountains could be operated only one at a time, his attendants signaled to have the water turned on as he approached each fountain. The king received visitors in the coppices and held celebrations and banquets. Nature lightened the burden of etiquette, making the garden a kind of isolated retreat, far from the palace with its gold, its cares, and its crowds.

Little is known of André Le Nôtre, creator of the gardens at Versailles, as he wrote almost nothing about his art. As the son of Louis XIII's chief gardener at the Tuileries, he spent his youth steeped in studies at the art studios in the palace of the Louvre. Le Nôtre began work as an architect and held the position of general supervisor of the royal buildings throughout his life. If he was knowledgeable in horticulture, he was first of all an architect, heir to the great tradition of "regularity" in the French garden bequeathed by

The Fountain of Latona covered with snow. According to Greek mythology, Zeus and the Titan Leto (called Latona by the Romans) conceived the twins Apollo and Artemis, who were born on the island of Ortygia. Balthazar and Gaspard Marsy carved the statues between 1668 and 1670.

the Middle Ages and the Renaissance. For the 7,400 acres of Versailles, he imagined myriad ways to achieve his intimidating goal of transforming a marshy plain into a luxurious landscape.

Incredibly, Le Nôtre designed the project in one year. It was immediately approved, and the work began with the aid of many scholars and engineers. The work went on continuously through the years but slowed during the 1670s owing to the insufficient water supply. It was taken up once more and revived under Louis XV for the Marble (Grand) Trianon, and again under Louis XVI for the Petit Trianon and the Queen's Hamlet. Thus the grounds experienced round after round of modifications. Abandoned during the French Revolution, then saved by Louis-Philippe, the gardens slowly assumed the look that we recognize today, but it is not exactly as Louis XIV would have wanted it. His Versailles was more richly colored, more pleasant, and more charming. Flowers and topiary shaped like chess pieces surrounded the plant beds, and beautifully scented plants and flowers in great terra-cotta pots appeared almost everywhere. The coppices played their secondary role as private sitting rooms as they shaded architectural structures, which were still visible above the trees lining the walkways.

Today the trees have become gigantic, storms have taken their toll, and one can only try to imagine the initial spirit of a garden that was never completed. Nevertheless, the Versailles of Le Nôtre remains the symbol of a garden art that is both disciplined and luminous and one that would inspire the world until the beginning of the twentieth century. A magnificent pleasure garden, aging Versailles has been transformed into a park of another era. In this culture that celebrated luxury and glory one can still perceive the nostalgia and the splendid dreams of a triumphant monarch.

The Fountain of Enceladus, a gilded lead sculpture made by Gaspard Marsy in 1670. In Greek mythology, Enceladus was a Titan punished for his revolt against the gods of Olympus by being buried under a mound of rocks, which became the island of Sicily.

Sculpture representing a river in one
of the fountains of the water garden

The waters of the Fountain of Apollo flow toward the Fountain of Latona between rows of yew trees shaped like cones and statues, now covered in tarpaulins for the winter.

France **Villandry**

As an adventure, Villandry is astonishing. This gleaming carpet of boxwood, flowers, and vegetable gardens nestled in the heart of the Loire Valley is the work of a Spanish doctor named Joachim Carvallo. Although nothing predisposed him to a love of gardens, he restored the château in just a few years and created incomparable gardens that thrill 400,000 visitors every year.

Above: In the garden of the crosses, a Maltese cross is represented in shaped boxwood. At its left is the Basque cross and at its right the cross of Languedoc.

Opposite: The château was restored to its Renaissance appearance by Dr. Joachim Carvallo, who began the huge task in 1906.

Built in the first half of the sixteenth century by Jean Le Breton, the powerful minister of finance under François I, Villandry is the last of the great châteaux of the Loire. Elegant, imposing, and well constructed, it is surrounded by steep sides, which do not, however, make the château a powerful fortress. A butte on the east, a plateau to the south, and the village of Villandry to the west form a kind of amphitheater that opens on the Cher Valley and encloses the gardens. To appreciate the design of the gardens, one must view them from the top of the dungeon or from the promenade that encircles this patchwork quilt of delights.

Born in Extramadura, Spain, in 1869, Dr. Carvallo went to Paris to work with Charles Richet, the Nobel Prize–winning physiologist. After a few years in Paris, Carvallo met an American student, Ann Coleman, whom he married in 1905. The Coleman family, which owned several steel mills, saw to the needs of the young family, who proceeded to look for a country house. Taken by the charm of the long-neglected residence of Villandry, they decided to settle in and put it back in shape.

This ambitious project turned out to be a gigantic enterprise. The château had been disfigured in the eighteenth century by the marquis de Castellane, who "modernized" it without restraint and turned the long-abandoned Renaissance garden into a park. After a brief interval under the ownership of Jérôme Bonaparte, it fell into the hands of a wealthy banker, who landscaped the grounds of his new residence in the English style.

Viewed from the height of the old dungeon, the canal that flows from the ancient Baroque pool separates the ornamental garden (left) and the vegetable garden (right).

The kitchen garden was modeled on the *potager* of the sixteenth century, when gardeners introduced new vegetables from the Americas. Some of these were featured in the drawings by Jacques Androuet du Cerceau that inspired Dr. Carvallo.

A wonderful selection of cabbages, chosen
for their shape as well as their color

Joachim Carvallo decided to restore Villandry to the way it had been in the sixteenth century. Although he could rely on old engravings of the buildings, the earliest layout he could find for the gardens was dated 1762. All that remained of the original installations were a reflecting pool of Baroque design and a canal feeding the moats that partially encircled the château and the outer courtyard. Carvallo retained this system, augmented it with a water garden centered on a great ornamental pond built by his son, and installed elegant waterfalls on the canal. The refreshing sound of splashing water added a lovely dimension to the otherwise geometric structure.

Carvallo's sources of inspiration for these gardens are more or less familiar to us today. It is thought that he relied heavily upon Claude Mollet's *Theatre of Agriculture* (1679); *A Treatise on Gardening* (1638) by Jacques Boyceau de la Baraudière, general steward of the royal gardens; and the drawings in Jacques Androuet du Cerceau's *Most Excellent Buildings in France* (1576). Carvallo also based his garden plan on those of the medieval monastery and its rigid designs, which were organized according to function into the cloister, the vegetable garden, the apothecary garden, and the fruit orchard. After removing the hundred-year-old cedars in the English park with dynamite, Carvallo graded the land and reestablished the terraces. With the help of a Spanish artist named Lozano, he proceeded to design the gardens of his dreams.

The ornamental gardens at Villandry are laid out in front of the salon windows. Dedicated to the theme of love, these gardens represent tender love, illustrated by hearts surrounded by flames; passionate love, represented by broken hearts; and tragic love, shown with swords and daggers. This imagery is accomplished with topiary of sculpted boxwood and flowers of flamboyant colors. Nearby, the garden of the crosses brings together various symbols around a stylized Maltese cross.

To the right of the canal, on the highest terrace, is the garden of music, in which lyres and harps of clipped boxwood are dominated by topiary in the form of chandeliers to "illuminate" the various sections. A bit farther along the canal, near the apothecary garden, stretches the renowned potager, or vegetable garden, where artichokes, eggplants, endive, pumpkins, carrots, and celery, among others, form a magical carpet of startling beauty. In wintertime, as one looks down from the dungeon, the red cabbages glisten like amethysts, the white cabbages resemble gilded pearls, and the leeks remind one of copper ornaments with a patina of verdigris.

Panorama: View of the kitchen garden. At the corners of the compartments, small arbors covered with roses offer shaded viewing areas.

Ambleville

Ambleville
FRANCE

The art of the garden is sensitive to prevailing tastes and fashion and to their cycles. So it was that interest in Italian gardens of the Renaissance was revived at the end of the nineteenth century after the restoration of the gardens at the Villa Gamberaia. When the marquise de Villefranche bought the estate of Ambleville in 1928, she wanted to surround her château with the gardens that its original owner, having just returned from Tuscany, would have imagined in the sixteenth century.

Above: An immense chessboard of narcissi blooms each spring in the Sun Garden.

Opposite: The hedgerow of greenery, or exedra, inspired by a painting by Andrea Mantegna. You can find similar shapes in many Italian villa and German park gardens.

In the Île-de-France, on a plateau called Le Vexin, is the lovely château of Ambleville. Partly built in the sixteenth century, the château belonged to Nicolas de Villeroy (1598–1685), the French ambassador to Florence, and he had the first fixtures and installations designed in the Italian style. The topography lent itself to the type of garden design that had inspired Mme de Villefranche at the Tuscan Villa Gamberaia. From the windows of the château, the Private Garden is first in the line of view, which overlooks the sunken Moon Garden, and finally a portico of sculpted yew trees. The scene is evocative of a painting of Andrea Mantegna at the Louvre, *Minerva Chasing Vice from the Garden of Virtue* (c. 1500), although similar settings are also found at Gamberaia and Versailles.

Each year Ambleville hosts special, glorious weeks in each season. In the spring, some 10,000 narcissi spring from the cold ground to create a giant chess board animated by topiary shaped like pawns. This gorgeous spectacle of nature takes place in the Sun Garden, which brings to mind the paintings of the Flemish painter Paul Brill (1524–1626). A little farther away, a giant serpent in boxwood slithers through the hundred-year-old foliage, and topiaries shaped like obelisks frame an ancient orange grove.

Ambleville is an island of elegance in a rustic landscape. Refined and inspired by literature, the gardens take us back to the era of French nobles who returned from the wars with Italy filled with new ideas and fresh images, and who opened the door to the French Renaissance.

The kitchen garden in winter's light with twenty-four plantings of tree peonies, mixed with winter blooming plants and tulips. At the left is a reservoir.

Following pages: In the middle of the Moon Garden, a pool acts as a mirror for a dancing figure of a boy.

Le Bois des Moutiers

Varengeville-sur-Mer

FRANCE

The park at Varengeville, classified as a historic monument in 1980, is one of the most exemplary creations of landscaping of the early twentieth century. The park and its gardens are also the fruit of two friendships—between the brilliant young architect Edwin Lutyens and Gertrude Jekyll, a designer of famous gardens, and between Lutyens and the Mallets, who sponsored the construction of this unique residence, a startling projection of British taste on the coast of Normandy.

Above: Beginning in 1898, the British architect Edwin Lutyens designed the manor house of the Bois des Moutiers attached to the existing dwelling.

Opposite: Gertrude Jekyll anticipated places for a visitor to pause and rest in order to contemplate the beauty of nature, to meditate, or to dream, as in Chinese or Japanese gardens.

Guillaume Mallet, scion of a family of Protestant bankers, spent his childhood in a château surrounded by grounds landscaped in the English style under the influence of the famous Scottish gardener Thomas Blaikie (1751–1838). Mallet then went on to live in the gentle climate of the Isle of Wight, of which he always bore fond memories, and eventually this dedicated Anglophile bought a grand house in Varengeville, near Dieppe, whose major assets consisted of thirty acres sloping down to the English Channel and the acidic ground conducive to garden plantings. His goal was to create a garden, but the house did not lend itself to the type of life envisioned by this bourgeois aesthete. When Mallet met Edwin Lutyens in Paris, he convinced the architect to visit Varengeville and subsequently hired him. At the time, Lutyens had just embarked on a career that would make him the preferred architect of high Edwardian society.

His style is not easily defined. He passed through an Arts and Crafts phase, inspired by reading John Ruskin, William Morris, and the architect Charles F. A. Voysey, and then he concentrated on brilliantly interpreting neoclassical styles. An extreme formalist, Lutyens was among the last and most eminent representatives of that inspired and idiosyncratic eclecticism that is the charm of British architecture. For the Mallets, he envisioned a magnificent manor supported in part by the old house. He cultivated asymmetry and took great advantage of the views of the countryside and of the sea. He altered traditional forms, such as the oriels that embellished the Romanesque entryway, and he added chimneys in the Voysey style to give the building an elegant height. The Bois des Moutiers is one of the most powerful and best-preserved examples of the Arts and Crafts style.

The border of the walkway that slopes down to the Iris Valley is planted in gunneras, huge Brazilian rhubarb plants, and giant rhododendrons.

For the garden and the grounds, Mallet called upon the talent of the celebrated Gertrude Jekyll, but he had very precise ideas as to what he wished to achieve. The great landscaper suffered from severe nearsightedness and could no longer travel, but she worked from her friend's plans according to a collaborative technique that they often practiced. Mallet was the enlightened client, Lutyens the passionate architect, and Jekyll the inspired gardener who chose the plantings.

The Bois des Moutiers is actually composed of two distinct parts, which Lutyens wisely separated by great walls to the entrance and around the gardens. These compartments created by the walls served a function other than that of beauty. They protected the exposed site from the dominant winds, and created a feeling of intimacy.

One approaches the house via a wide brick walkway between two high walls, at the base of which are planted mixed borders full of vitality and typical of Jekyll's style. The walkway ends in a circular forecourt formerly framed by four cypress trees, although only two stand there today. There are two openings on each side, their vaults emphasized with radiating bricks, with one side looking out on a rose garden, formerly the White Garden. The other opening looks out upon a long pergola thick with vines and roses; it once led to an enclosed vegetable garden, which is today a rose garden. Just a bit farther away lies a terrace by the sea, which offers romantic views of both the sea and the landscaped grounds.

The park follows next. To the left of the house stretches the Grazing Ground, an ancient moor sown in grass and planted with pines, azaleas, holly, and large-leafed rhododendrons. There is also a cherry grove that was replanted after a recent storm, and a walkway lined with Himalayan rhododendrons. The Great Park then slowly descends toward the English Channel, and here is one of the most beautiful walks one can find in this region of France. The Iris Valley, the Glade of Japanese Cedars, the Knoll of Yulan Magnolias, the Camellia Allée, and the Azalea Walk all feature clever compositions, as well as colors and textures. Here one finds *halopeanum* rhododendrons, which have grown eleven feet tall in the sea air; hydrangeas; huge magnolias; ferns interspersed with great azaleas; bald cypress trees with their feathery leaves; and hundreds of plants that Guillaume Mallet imported from around the world.

The Bois des Moutiers does not look exactly as it did in the 1920s, because the coast of Dieppe is subject to horrific storms and it has been necessary to replace uprooted trees or those ripped apart by the wind, but the Mallet family has kept the same passionate interest in this exceptional place. A century after the first plantings, the Bois des Moutiers has known how to respect the spirit of its creators—a fine amateur, a grand architect, and a great maker of gardens.

An entrance to one of the enclosed gardens. The stairway design is typical of the careful attention that Lutyens gave to areas of transition.

In the park, the Azalea Walk
ends in an explosion of white pearl
rhododendron, a pretty hybrid
distinguished by the red color in the
throat of the flower.

Giverny

After discovering the landscapes of the Normandy coast or the Île-de-France, the polders of Holland, or the streets of London and Rouen, Claude Monet returned from his travels to retire to a house at Giverny on the banks of the Epte River. Within a few years, he had created a natural fairyland, one of the only artist's gardens that remain from an era when nature was rediscovered in painting and in the decorative arts with passion and intensity.

Above: White wisteria drapes over the Japanese bridge that Claude Monet installed in the water garden he began in 1893: "a charming thing, a motif to paint."

Opposite: Claude Monet's house in front of the Norman Garden, seen from the water garden

It was in 1883 that Monet left his charming but crumbling house in Argenteuil, where amid the flowers he had welcomed Renoir, Manet, Pissarro, and Caillebotte, who lived across the Seine. The Impressionist group had dispersed by then, and even though the ties of friendship were still strong, each artist followed his own road from then on.

Until his death, Monet always painted what he felt. He called upon his technical virtuosity to convey the subtlest of sensations. Without a preconceived system, he used broad strokes, stippling, small patches, or large expanses of color, as well as textures both heavy and thin. His only guide was the effect of light on is subject.

He began to be recognized in the 1880s, and he emerged from the state of near poverty that he had experienced since his youth. At Giverny he rented a large house that was somewhat dilapidated, and it was there that he commenced the second half of his life.

Built on a hillside bordering a small river, the house was well situated, although somewhat isolated. A train would occasionally pass through on the railroad tracks at the end of the garden, but its path barely ruffled the calm of the place. Once Monet outfitted the house, he looked to the garden. Without any special gardening knowledge and in spite of the fact that he disliked the classical French garden style, Monet designed his garden in the form of a functional rectangle with long, narrow flower beds divided by gravel paths. To this he gave his personal contribution of flora in profusion. The plants and flowers were so tightly planted that a visitor, Stephen Gwynn, remarked that "one could not insert his hand between them." The flowers were common varieties—tulips, daffodils, digitalis, lilies, bellflowers, daisies, and marigolds—but the closeness of

The Norman Garden, planted in rectangular beds, bursts with innumerable bulbous flowers. Monet mixed common plants with both wild and rare species.

their blooms created a wild stream of blurry color, one that is depicted in Monet's well-known painting *The Garden of Giverny* (1895). Two large grassy rectangles were planted in the orchards, and the path to the entryway was lined with arches painted in "Monet green." Soon these were completely covered with roses and clematis, which grew beautifully entwined. Little by little, gardening became the master's second passion, and he enjoyed composing and recomposing this natural scene, which soon became one of his principal subjects.

Monet had found success in the field of art collecting, and by 1890 he could afford to buy the house. In 1893 he added the land that faced the house, as well as the parcels beyond the road and the railroad tracks. His friend Georges Clemenceau later wrote: "Monet is the only painter with a railroad in his garden." Monet the gardener set himself a new goal: Transform all the fields into a garden-studio, with a water garden like those he had admired in prints, in the accounts of travelers, and in photographs. He quickly had the first pool dug and supplied it with water diverted from the river. There he introduced his first water lilies, to the annoyance of the locals, who feared that these foreign plants would poison their water. Monet soon enlarged the pool, which become a pond, and built a Japanese bridge over it. This was followed by a second bridge, and then came the wisteria, which is still there today, along with bamboo and weeping willows. Within a few years, he had created the scenes of nature he had always wanted to paint. He knew instinctively that this compressed world, this fusion of water, earth, trees, and flowers, would lead to the conclusion of his final work, the immense *Water Lilies* in the Musée de l'Orangerie in the Tuileries gardens.

After Monet's death in 1926, his son occupied Giverny for several years, but it was virtually abandoned after World War II. Given by his son to the Académie des Beaux-Arts, the house and gardens were saved by an energetic restoration campaign funded largely by Americans. The gardens were restored from 1974 to 1976, and one regrets a bit that the restorers did not keep the same plants that Monet had chosen with such care. The main house, the studios, the Norman Garden, and the Water Garden welcome more than 500,000 visitors each year. Claude Monet always loved company.

Panorama: Water lilies in the garden pond; the recently rebuilt Japanese bridge is visible at the back.

Apremont Floral Park

FRANCE

Apremont-
sur-Allier

Subjected to the rhythm of the seasons, the carefully tended gardens of Apremont are protected from the rigors of the weather. They change with every passing year, all the while trying to circumvent the gardener's will, and each spring they awaken to a new beauty. Who today can imagine that in 1970 cows still grazed peacefully on what has become one of the most beautiful gardens of central France, the Apremont Floral Park?

Above: The White Garden, inspired by Vita Sackville-West's
Sissinghurst garden, with its obelisks of sculpted yew trees

Opposite: Multicolored mixed border near the outbuildings

A few miles from the city of Nevers, on the edge of the province of Allier, is located an estate that has been in the same family since the eighteenth century. Through marriage, Apremont came to be owned by Eugène Schneider, a master of the forge, who loved the château and the village so much that he restored them both over the course of fifty years. His grandson, Gilles de Brissac, decided in 1970 to create this garden, which opened to the public in 1977.

Although its effects are invisible today, heavy construction was required to dam a small valley in order to redirect water toward a series of ponds and to move 600 tons of rock to install a waterfall. The gardens, which link the château to the old village, were not conceived according to one particular style, a fact that only contributes to their charm.

The gardens at Apremont are a product of the imagination of a cultivated man, and one finds here allusions to eighteenth-century park design and to Italian topiary art, as well as to Sissinghurst Castle in Kent, England, and its White Garden inspired by Gertrude Jekyll. A Chinese bridge, designed by the watercolorist and decorator Juan de Besteigui; a Turkish pavilion at the edge of the water conceived by Alexandre Serebriakoff; and a belvedere decorated with ceramic plaques depicting scenes of Nevers all contribute to a joyful atmosphere amid the rustic luxuriance of vegetation. The plant beds are lush, and the flowers, both annuals and perennials, are so hardy that they spill over the edges of the mixed borders. Likewise, few visitors are likely to forget the *allée* of white wisteria or the sparkling colors of the park in the fall.

The Chinese bridge, designed by
Juan de Besteigui to resemble an
eighteenth-century garden folly

Levens Hall

In the cold beauty of the Lake District of northwest England lies one of the masterpieces of European topiary art. Designed by a French gardener in the seventeenth century and rescued by an Englishman in the nineteenth, the gardens of Levens Hall found their salvation by opening to the public, but without losing a bit of their extravagance.

Above: The arched entryway to the garden, topped with a royal crown

Opposite: The topiary garden surrounding Levens Hall, a sixteenth-century manor house, was replanted at the beginning of the nineteenth century, according to a 1730 garden inventory.

In his famous *Journal* and in his letters, Samuel Pepys mentions highly placed people who, once they had made their fortune or in order to escape political turmoil, retired to the countryside. Such was the case of the privy purse to King James II, Colonel James Grahme, who moved in 1688 into the huge Elizabethan residence of Levens Hall, a mansion that was graced with charm, if not comfort. He immediately set about modernizing the buildings and redesigning the park and the gardens. For this he commissioned Guillaume Beaumont, a student of landscape architect André Le Nôtre. Beaumont had participated in the creation of the gardens of Hampton Court, which were considered remarkable in that era and are still beloved in ours. From 1694 onward, Beaumont gave his undivided attention to what would become one of the most beautiful parks in this outlying region of the kingdom.

Considered on their own merits, Beaumont's park, his garden of ancient plants, *allées* of three-hundred-year-old beech trees, rose garden, and ornamental vegetables are each worth a visit; yet it is the topiary garden that particularly fascinates the thousands of visitors who come annually to Levens Hall. According to the author of *Jardin, Vocabulaire typologique et technique* (1999), the art of topiary consists in "directing the sap of a straight, evergreen plant, or a herbaceous plant by clipping, wiring, and sometimes grafting in order to realize sculptured plants." This involves a direct intervention in—or against—the nature of the plant, with the aid of clipping and pruning, of supports, and even of weights to shape the form of an animal, an object, or another plant. This art, which we can compare to bonsai or to the Japanese art of *o-karikomi*, has been practiced in Europe since antiquity. One can also find examples of topiary in medieval

In the topiary garden, the bushes and trees take the form of chess pawns, animals, and geometric figures, among others. The center tree has been called one of the fifty most beautiful trees in Britain.

tapestries and illuminations. Topiary was practiced mainly in Italy during the Renaissance but it soon became more widely appreciated throughout Europe by the sixteenth and seventeenth centuries. A "tamed" plant, one that is well formed and symmetrical, or that is transformed into a statue, fits in perfectly with the French philosophy of the classic garden. The return to nature in the eighteenth and nineteenth centuries removed such heavy-handedness from view, but topiary made a discreet return in the gardens of the Edwardians and then came back in force at the beginning of the twentieth century. Certain contemporary designers (at the Tuileries gardens, for example) have taken an interest in this form, which is once again fresh and new, but in a modified, less extreme form.

Levens Hall has attained its unique place in history because of the quantity and density of its topiary, a garden extravaganza barely tempered by Beaumont's formal French-style layout. Chess pieces, spirals, parasols, lions, peacocks, chickens, pyramids, spheres and half-spheres, a crown, and even a representation of Queen Elizabeth I rub shoulders with one another. All this life continues under the strict rule of the clippers and four implacable gardeners.

The garden did not always look like this. At the beginning of the nineteenth century, the choice of flowers was modernized, and the topiary almost disappeared. About 1810 the gardener Alexander Forbes had replanted or resculpted them according to a very precise inventory of the garden that had been taken in 1730. Today these gardens are an exceptional example of a refined art that has always enthralled amateur gardeners and has now spread throughout the world, albeit on a more modest level. Located not far from the Kent river, at the edge of a marvelous region for tourism, Levens Hall merits a long visit.

The green and golden yews and the boxwood have been sculpted for many years to achieve these somewhat disquieting shapes.

Stourhead

"We were all born in Arcadia," wrote Arthur Schopenhauer *in his Art of Being Happy. We all strive for happiness, but it takes us many long years to realize that it is but a fragile concept, and often just a mere fantasy. Even when we know it, we still endeavor to attain this ideal. Happiness must have been the dream of Henry Hoare, who returned to England, dazzled by his Grand Tour of Italy, and created Stourhead, one of the most magnificent English gardens of the eighteenth century.*

Above: View of the lake around which Stourhead Park was organized in the eighteenth century

Opposite: The Temple of Apollo, constructed in 1765, is one of many picturesque buildings that enliven the landscape.

A brand-new art of gardening has just been introduced: it is so popular. . .that we are redesigning all the great parks and gardens in the kingdom to henceforth follow the ideas of Mr. Kent, that is, without terracing or straight lines." This remark was made in 1734 by Sir Thomas Robinson, a diplomat and great amateur gardener, to convey the swing in garden design occurring in England at the time. Great Britain had defeated Louis XIV at Blenheim in 1704; the English agricultural reform was beginning to bear fruit; and the country had already taken the first steps to industrialization. Amassing great wealth, England conquered vast territories in Africa, North America, Asia, and Oceania, and was becoming the primary power in Europe. While the European continent still labored under absolutism, Great Britain would soon recognize the virtues of liberalism as defined by Adam Smith. In science, John Locke shone light on human perception while Linnaeus proposed "a system of nature," and in his *Species plantarum* opened the door to the modern study of botany. The competition that exists in the heart of nature was seen as legitimizing that which rules among men and in economic matters. The garden *à la française* with its complex patterns, gravel pathways, and topiary could not appeal to the enlightened high society of Britain.

Eighteenth-century England also saw the initiation and development of huge agricultural tracts of land. Money was available, but opportunities to multiply it without undue risk remained rare. Thus, investing in land became the economic opportunity of the day, and it was practiced on a grand scale. By this means, the bank of Sir Richard Hoare acquired the estate of Stourton in 1717. Henry Hoare inherited Stourton in 1720 and passed it to his son, Henry Hoare II, "the Magnificent." After taking a Grand Tour of Italy, where he discovered the pastoral landscapes of Claude Lorrain and Gaspard Dughet, the younger Henry decided to make his home at Stourton, which he renamed Stourhead Park. In 1745, with the architect Henry Flitcroft, Henry Hoare undertook the building of a park of ninety-nine acres within an estate of more than eleven thousand.

The old Stourton house, ruined since 1718, was replaced with a residence designed by Colin Campbell based on Palladio's Villa Elmo. The facade faces a wide valley dotted with a string of ponds fed by the Stour river. Hoare's ingenious idea was to integrate these ponds into an enormous lake that would be the focal point of his park. This idea did not come out of the blue, however. A cultivated man, Hoare was well informed of the transformations wrought upon the lands of his wealthy friends and clients; he too took a grand view and encompassed the totality of the landscape in his project. The borders between the park and the agricultural land were vague, almost invisible. The circuit walk contained surprises with each turn, just like a natural landscape,

Opposite: The grotto, built about 1755 and dedicated to Aeneas, contains several marble statues, one of which is this *Sleeping Naiad.* Part of the ceiling is decorated with seashells.

Nymph of the grot these sacred springs I keep,
And to the murmur of these waters sleep;
Ah spare my slumbers, gently tread the cave,
And drink in silence or in silence lave. A. Pope

but at a much more regular pace and at interesting angles created by the V shape of the lake. Over the years, Hoare added an obelisk, a grotto, an elegant pantheon, a waterfall, a stone archway, a temple to Apollo, a tunnel, and a temple to the goddess Flora. Later on, he brought the medieval Bristol Cross to Stourhead, saving one of England's architectural treasures from destruction. He also built a neo-Gothic cottage and refurbished the village of Stourton.

For aristocrats who often led a sedentary life, a walk in the park was one of the high points of a visit to a country house. The host and his guests would explore the park's circuit on foot, on horseback, or by carriage. The landscape drawings prepared for clients by William Kent, who had studied architecture and landscape in Italy, often feature imagined scenes—people listening to a concert in a miniature temple, sipping drinks on an island accessible only by boat, bathing in a Roman-style bath house. Most often, people were pictured engaging in the gentle art of conversation or cloistered with a good book in a pagoda or rotunda, on a bench, or in a cool grotto.

The ties between painting and the representation of nature at Stourhead were very strong. The Pantheon designed by Flitcroft for the estate was inspired by Lorrain's painting *Landscape with Aeneas at Delos*, and Henry Hoare, himself a fine amateur of Italian-style paintings, wrote that the view of his village made "a charming painting in the style of Gaspard [Dughet]." Literature, too, was represented in the park, hence the many allusions to the voyage of Aeneas after the fall of Troy, particularly the inscriptions on the monuments.

Life at Stourhead must have been very pleasant in this luxurious landscape that was at once natural and unreal. The park that one visits today is not the one built by Henry Hoare II. In 1785 Richard Colt Hoare made many modifications. He removed some of the novelties, including the Turkish tent, a Chinese alcove, a fanciful Venetian construction, and an orange grove. He dispensed with a bridge, knocked down some cottages that blocked a view of the village church, and added crenellation to the remaining houses and the clock tower. There were additions, too, including a Tudor-style pavilion for the groundskeeper and a second lake. The park's new owner completely transformed the system of *allées* and paths and moved the entrance to a new location.

Until Richard Colt Hoare's renovations, the trees were deliberately kept at a distance, which gave the views an airy transparence of the type seen in prints and paintings of the day. Richard Colt introduced the invasive laurel tree and such exotic plants as the giant rhododendron. With its overabundance of trees today, Stourhead has lost some of its light and airiness, but this is ever the lot of parks and gardens: nature always tries to reclaim its rights. Still, the creation of Henry Hoare II justly remains the most admirable of those parks that brought forth the English style.

Panorama: Views of the lake, which was inspired by paintings by Claude Lorrain

Little Sparta

Scotland

UNITED KINGDOM

Robert Louis Stevenson described Edinburgh as "the Athens of the North," a title that prompted the poet and landscape artist Ian Hamilton Finlay to call his garden Little Sparta. Finlay fashioned his garden from a piece of property called Stonypath he bought at Lanark, not far from Edinburgh, and made it into a retreat sheltered from a world that was a bit too modern for his taste.

Above: The upper pond at Little Sparta is fed by water run-off. At the left is an Ionic capital, a nostalgic and poetic touch that inspires one to reflect on the end of *civilization*.

Opposite: A quotation from Louis Saint-Just—"The order of today is the disorder of tomorrow"—engraved in stone expresses one of the ideas behind the creation of poet, sculptor, and gardener Ian Hamiliton Finlay.

Finlay is first of all a poet, one of the British members of a movement called Concrete Poetry, which appeared after World War II. Heir to Dada, cousin of Lettrism, Concrete Poetry employs more than words; it may incorporate graphics, sounds, even objects. Obstinate and sometimes provocative, Finlay, whose political opinions were judged ambiguous by some, denounced in both his work and his statements the loss of cultural references. As he had little respect for the avant-garde, which he considered subsidized art, he incurred the deep hostility of the art establishment.

In a dozen years, this poem-garden created on a windswept moor achieved the appearance we recognize today. In this work, Finlay suggests a journey across the history of ideas by means of an overwhelming multitude of cultural references. These may be presented as ancient-style inscriptions and sculptures, or as alterations of buildings or signs, or as progressions. Thus a bridge bears the Latin word *Claudi* over its arch in commemoration of Claude Lorrain, whose landscapes resemble the scene viewed from the top of the bridge. A quotation from Louis Saint-Just engraved in stone reads, "The world is empty since the Romans," which is one of many elements that recall the philosophy of the French Revolution. A birdbath made in the shape of an aircraft carrier on which birds make a "landing," is one of the numerous allusions to the military. One of these is an urn that looks like a hand grenade, a symbol of the cultural war, the artist's task of "classical rearmament," and the threat of destruction.

One would not stroll through Little Sparta as one would in the lush, scented gardens of a Tuscan villa. There is nothing pleasant in the austere plantings supported by this rigorous climate, nothing historical about the place. Rather, it is a philosophical discourse that leads the visitor into its intellectual entrenchments, to sometimes disturb, or to entice.

On the Scottish moors, Ian Hamilton Finlay also asks a basic question: "What is the purpose of a garden?" Is it to create beauty, to display a vision of the world, to reveal nature, or to prove that one is its master? In its rambling way, Little Sparta proposes an answer whose origins go back nearly to the Garden of Eden: a garden is the image of the world. Little Sparta, the image of a committed poet.

Finlay took a profound interest in the theoreticians of the French Revolution. Here is another quotation from Saint-Just: "The world has been empty since the Romans."

Head of Apollo. In another part of the
garden is a temple dedicated to the
Greek god: "To Apollo, his music, his
missiles, his muses."

Tortoise-tank. Allusions to war, in particular World War II, are prevalent throughout Little Sparta, including birdbaths made to resemble aircraft carriers and this tortoise sculpture bearing the legend "Panzer Leader," is probably a reference to the memoirs published with that title by the German General Heinz Guderian.

Sissinghurst Castle

UNITED KINGDOM

Cranbrook

Thanks to their charm and much to the personality of their creators, Sissinghurst Castle Gardens, designed just before World War II, are one of the most famous gardens in England. Because the writer Vita Sackville-West was taken with a passion for gardening, wrote about gardens, conducted garden conferences, and lectured on the topic for the BBC, Sissinghurst became a model that continues to inspire landscape gardeners today.

Above: View of the Moat Walk and the sixteenth-century tower where Vita Sackville-West had her study

Opposite: The famous White Garden, probably inspired by Muslim gardens. The roses are *Rosa mulliganii.*

Sissinghurst is a tale of an extraordinary woman, Victoria (Vita) Sackville-West (1892–1962). Lively, intelligent, and precocious, she was raised amid the munificence and splendor of Edwardian aristocracy, and by age eighteen she had already written many poems and several novels. In 1913 she married a brilliant diplomat, Harold Nicolson, who told her not long afterward of his bisexuality, a revelation that liberated her own sexual inclinations. Although they lived apart most of the time, the thousands of letters they exchanged constitute one of the great correspondences of the twentieth century.

In 1930 at the age of thirty-eight, tired of her life in high society and bothered by the opening of a chicken farm near her beautiful house at Long Barn, she discovered by chance an ancient, ruined manor that was for sale, Sissinghurst Castle. Harold came from London to see the place, and he too fell captive to its charm, so they decided to buy it. What they bought was the most recent structure on an ancient site, a run-down castle from the 1500s built on a ridge overlooking the Vale of Kent. Sissinghurst had lost its grandeur after it was neglected and was eventually turned into a farm. When Vita and Harold acquired the estate, there remained a rather imposing tower with two octagonal turrets; a long building that served as a stable and as housing for the farm workers; and two houses in the Tudor style, whose former beauty was in ruin.

One of the reasons for obtaining the property was the *possibility* of creating a garden at Sissinghurst, a word that the famous landscape designer Lancelot Brown (1716–1783) misused as *capability* when trying to convince his clients of the hidden virtues of their land. Vita and Harold both loved nature, and they had already lived in historic houses surrounded by gardens and beautiful grounds and had planted a dense garden at Long Barn in which the architect Edwin Lutyens, a close friend of garden designer Gertrude Jekyll and of Vita's mother, tried to instill a bit of order. Both Vita and Harold shared the tastes of their class. Where gardens were concerned, William Morris (1834–1896), the founder of the Arts and Crafts movement, described their view quite well: "[A garden] should be well fenced from the outside world. It should by no means imitate either the willfulness or the wildness of nature. It should in fact look like a part of the house." Another designer in vogue at the time, Reginald Blomfield, defended the concept of the compartmentalized garden, composed of pieces separated by paths, hedges, and walls.

Harold designed the layout of the garden from the vantage point of the top of the tower. He shouted instructions down to their two sons, Benedict and Nigel, who traipsed back and forth with pennants mounted on sticks to choose the perspectives and mark the alignments. The goal was to give unity and order to seven-and-a-half acres of land where none existed before. The

buildings, which Jekyll felt gave the garden its meaning, were still there, but dispersed and dissimilar. They are now the focal points of the garden's composition. The digging and grading of the land uncovered two sides of an ancient moat, providing for the creation of an ornamental lake; and a beautiful old wall that would serve as a crown for urns copied from those at Bagatelle.

Vita continued with their project. "A combination of long, straight walkways extending toward the four main intersections, each ending at a point of visual interest, such as a statue, two Italian poplars." And beyond these, the parts should be "like the rooms of an enormous house that open out onto the corridors." The walkways, the individual gardens, the water elements, a columned loggia, a statue of Dionysus, and the integration of the buildings are all significant, but the secret of the success of Sissinghurst is found in the balance between the formality of the design and the poetic sumptuousness and freedom of Vita's plantings. Soon she concentrated all her activity on her garden, and she continued to do so until her death in 1962. Dressed in riding pants, boots, flannel shirt, straw hat, and pearls, and assisted by three gardeners, she engaged in the myriad activities that create and enrich a true garden. The plants that she ordered from all over Great Britain or brought back from her trips abroad amplified the rich color harmonies from year to year. All the while, she continued to write novels and publish poems, write a regular gardening column for the newspaper *The Observer*, give conferences, and host a regular broadcast on the BBC. She raised her sons and traveled throughout Europe, managed the complex family finances, and came to the aid of her friends. During World War II, she drove her Buick as an ambulance. During all this intense activity and unbeknownst to her, she formalized a style—"the new picturesque"—that would be emulated throughout England. In 1938 she opened Sissinghurst to the public and received visitors with pleasure. Thanks to this indefatigable activity, ancient varieties of roses bloom once more, just as they do at Sissinghurst; monochromatic gardens are seen throughout Great Britain and Europe; and climbing roses use the trunks of trees as natural trellises.

It was not Vita and Harold's intention to create a monument or a model garden but rather to relive the beautiful memories of their childhood. Most of all, it is probably the project through which they were finally able to find themselves. In some measure, this dream they held in common compensated for the suffering of their troubled lives.

Visitors to the garden should not forego a visit to the top of the tower, where they can appreciate the garden from the perspective where it was conceived. During the visit, one can see Vita's study, a beautiful room stacked with books, about a hundred of which came from her pen or Harold's.

Panorama: Seen from the top of the tower are the cottage, the rose garden, and in the foreground, the alley of yews.

Portrack House

Man has always looked for meaning in his relationship with nature. The gardens of the Middle Ages represented the Garden of Eden and man's desire to return there. Those of the Renaissance took their symbolism from classical antiquity. The seventeenth and eighteenth centuries were also imbued with mythological references until the idea of art for art's sake, and horticultural theories took the upper hand. The modern garden has retained the artistic approach, and Charles Jencks's "garden of cosmic speculation" is one of the most spectacular examples.

Above: A graphic and sculptural reconstruction of the landscape, defined by the snake mound at the left and the snail mound at the right

Opposite: The Galactic Bench in the Garden of Physics

The architect Charles Jencks is one of the principal theoreticians of style of postmodern architecture about which we heard so much during the 1970s. In reaction to modernism, which was looked upon as inhuman, postmodernism contributed to the culture and hence to history, which is one of the fundamental elements of architectural theory. Critics of Jencks's creations either praised his creativity as authentic or dismissed it as simply rearranging old forms. It is indeed interesting to see what Jencks did with the idea of the garden.

In southern Scotland, Jencks found the ideal land for his experiment. The forty acres of land was part of a tract owned by his wife, Lady Keswick, a specialist in the art of the Chinese garden. Between 1990 and 2000, Jencks created a surprising landscape that mixes many centuries of gardening and the sciences. His approach stemmed from the concept of chaos and that of a complex nature whose forms are perpetually evolving. This evolution follows a dynamic that is not linear, but rather cosmological. To this theoretical base were added certain principles of geomancy, the ancient Chinese art of divination, which has merged with feng shui, a subject that fascinated Maggie Keswick long before it became well known in the West.

The garden is divided into several very different zones, including a spectacular cascade of the universe, all in concrete, stemming from a basin that illustrates a "quark soup," and thus the origin of the world. There is the Garden of Physics, with its spiral DNAlike mound that encloses a kind of chapel of Op art; an immense burial mound in the form of a serpent; and lakes of complex twists and turns. One passes well-ordered plant beds divided by paths lined in boxwood; a science-fiction landscape planted in turf; and then a walkway, made of thin wooden slats, which leads to the Jumping Bridge. The meanings evoked by the garden sculpture are quite literal, such as the enormous silvery mouth posed sensually over a bed of red strawberries, or the double helix of DNA that springs from the ground.

Jencks used the landscape as a raw material to work his concept of cosmology into an inspired collage. His speculations on the cosmos, their metaphors, and their occasional humor certainly reach out to the visitors. Those who are willing to play take great pleasure in identifying the symbolic forms and the sculptures, like strollers in the eighteenth century beholding the rock garden at Sanspareil. Contemporary in the extreme, Portrack House is nonetheless filled with a great nostalgia for the gardens of yesteryear.

In the Garden of Physics, a double helix illustrates the structure of a DNA molecule. At the base this structure is a female head, a symbol of intuition.

A terrace made of lawn and concrete
symbolizing the loss of all matter into
the black hole of space, where gravity
bends light to nothing

The Jumping Bridge is inspired by the
catastrophe theory, which maintains
that a small modification can provoke
massive changes.

Belgium Freÿr

Thanks to the efforts of at least twenty generations of a single family, the astonishing ensemble unifying a fifteenth- to sixteenth-century château and its seventeenth-century gardens has come down to us mostly intact. Some of the famous orange trees of Freÿr that were purchased at the court of Lorraine in the eighteenth century are still blooming after more than three hundred years.

Above: The château and its gardens, seen from a cliff on the opposite bank of the Meuse River

Opposite: View of the arbor and the high cliffs of Freÿr

Most of the gardens in the French style were designed for open landscapes, but not at Freÿr, which is located near Dinant, at the edge of the Belgian Ardennes forest. The deep forest surrounds the château, which was built on the floor of the Meuse Valley, in an area hemmed in by cliffs more than 330 feet high.

In the eighteenth century, the château was refitted for use as a summer home for the dukes of Beaufort-Spontin. After 1760 its Renaissance gardens were redesigned according to a classical plan, one that would be in harmony with the rigorous architecture. The gardens extend for more than seven acres along the Meuse River on both sides of the château. The design alternates pools with water jets, quincuncial arrangements of lime trees, and two large ornamental lakes around which stand thirty-three boxed orange trees, cared for with unwavering dedication for more than 250 years. In line with the central pool, a perpendicular *allée* leads to the second part of the garden, which was built at a slight angle, presumably to take advantage of what little sunshine there is. At the highest point stands a magnificent pavilion, built in the style of Louis XVI and overlooking a composition in two parts— tree-covered walkways and little groves of lime trees sculpted into the characters of playing cards.

In this somber countryside at the foot of the menacing cliffs, the gardens of Freÿr illustrate, albeit unintentionally, the contrast of our own garden creations with nature in the wild, and of a classicism about to give way to romanticism.

The great oval pool was installed at the end of the eighteenth century by Philippe de Beaufort-Spontin during his expansion of the gardens.

Schwetzingen

Although deeply influenced by Versailles, the style of living of the German aristocracy, which remained the ruling class almost to the end of the nineteenth century, had its own particular grandeur. If Voltaire's dying wish was to see Schwetzingen once more, the château and its grounds must have been extraordinary. This Baroque ensemble was left untouched by the devastating wars, and continues to be maintained by the state of Baden-Württemberg.

The name of Carl-Theodor (1724–1799), elector palatine and then king of Bavaria beginning in 1758, remains inseparable from Schwetzingen. To escape from life at his enormous palace of Mannheim, largely inspired by Versailles, he would retreat to Schwetzingen, an ancient castle used as a hunting lodge, which he transformed into a residence worthy of his rank. From 1748 to 1761, this cultivated king and aesthete enlarged the building with two *Zirkusgebaüden*, large wings in the shape of a semicircle that were the work of Alessandro Galli da Bibiena and Franz Rabaliatti. (This architectural form, new to the seventeenth century, would be taken up by the architect John Woods and his son at Bath a few years later.) Between these two elegant arms, the gardener, Johann Ludwig Petri, built a huge, circular garden, the first of its kind. Europe had seen gardens planted in a semicircle, such as Hampton Court, but the full circle was original. The idea was so pleasing that the prince asked one of the great French architects of the time, Nicolas de Pigage (1723–1796), who had built the Rococo theater for the château, to design gardens based on Petri's foundation.

Pigage, who had worked for Stanilas Leszczynski at Lunéville, was called upon throughout a period of nearly forty years in the development of the gardens of Schwetzingen, the masterpiece of this unjustly forgotten architect. He redesigned the plant beds, completed the semicircle with two quarters of trellis work, and, thanks to a complex puzzle of squares and rectangles, tripled the surface of the garden. At the end, he designed a majestic pool, whose beautiful reflections diverted everyone's gaze to the mountains in the distance. The concept of a garden in plant beds was that of the high French style and otherwise seemed inspired by *Théorie et pratique du jardinage*, a famous 1709 book attributed to Jean-Baptiste Le Blond, the creator of the gardens at Peterhof. The precise nature of the design did not preclude many attractive innovations in the plantings, such as paths bordered with lime trees that

The Grotto of Apollo looks toward the Theater of Greenery and the town of Schwetzingen.

provided shade and coolness in the summer, or the huge beds with so many trees they reminded one of labyrinths. Pigage used his grand imagination to design many works and fantasies, such as the bathhouse, a Chinese tea room, and a theater of greenery. He continued with such flights of fancy as a temple to Minerva made to appear in ruins, a Roman aqueduct, a temple to Mercury, and especially surprising, a "mosque" with two minarets. This last demonstrated an imagination and spirit that were not without links to the decorative painting of the era. The famous fountain of birds, which Pigage bought at Lunéville, marks the height of this picturesque art.

The construction slowed somewhat when Carl-Theodor left for Munich, but it picked up again as soon as he became interested in English gardens. He gave the responsibility of transforming Schwetzingen to Ludwig von Sckell (1750–1823), the most famous landscape architect in Germany. Von Sckell was so convinced of the value of Pigage's work that he refused to eliminate it. Such modesty became a stroke of genius, for he contented himself with creating grounds in the English style around the perimeter of the existing gardens, which by then extended to 185 acres. In the nineteenth century, Johann Michael Zeyer (1770–1843) deftly transformed the grand pool into a great romantic pond, and thus Baden-Württemberg possesses today an extraordinary ensemble that is a summation of garden art from the beginning of the seventeenth century to the middle of the nineteenth, with no designer having sacrificed the treasures of his predecessors.

Schwetzingen is a great historic garden that is perfectly preserved. It combines the precision of the French garden with the poetry of English landscaping, while incorporating all the elements of a great seventeenth-century work of art, from the sublime to the fantastic.

This romantic lake was made from an existing Baroque pool in the nineteenth century by the great German gardener Johann Michael Zeyer.

This little winding canal serves as a
birdbath.

The Fountain of the Birds. Originally belonging to the château of Malgrange, near Nancy, this fountain was purchased by Carl-Theodor during the estate sale of Stanislas Leszczynski, duke of Lorraine. At the back is a trompe l'œil entitled *The End of the World*.

Sanspareil

Montplaisir at Peterhof, Sans-Souci in Potsdam, Monbijou in Berlin, Sanspareil in Bayreuth—when the courts of Europe spoke French, these were the names the princes gave to their smaller residences. The margrave of Bayreuth, Wilhelmine, went even further by taking as the theme for her new gardens the Adventures of Telemachus *by Archbishop François de Salignac de la Mothe Fénelon, one of the most celebrated French literary works of the eighteenth century.*

Wilhelmine (1709–1758) was the eldest daughter of Friedrich Wilhelm of Prussia, the "soldier king," and the sister of Friedrich Wilhelm II (Frederick the Great). The family almost married her to a cousin, the future king of England, but finally gave her to Friedrich von Brandenburg-Bayreuth, son of the margrave of Bayreuth. Intelligent and cultivated, Wilhelmine is now remembered for her memoirs, which were written with an astonishing candor. Readers are amused by the description of her arrival at the Court of Bayreuth after her marriage: "They all had the kind of faces that would frighten small children. . .their mismatched features were rigged out in get-ups that had nothing on the lice for their age." She was extremely bored in Franconia, and writing her memoirs, which ended in 1742, was an outlet for her, or perhaps a way to strike back at a world that had been cruel to her.

"I am pleased with the perseverance with which death pursues the old margrave," wrote Friedrich II to his sister. With her father finally buried, Wilhelmine's husband launched into a program of building and modernizing his estates. This included a hospital, some town planning, a Rococo theater designed by Giuseppe Galli di Bibiena (the architect of Schwetzingen), the Hermitage Gardens at Bayreuth (which owed a great deal to her), and Sanspareil. In the Franconian Alps, about nineteen miles from Bayreuth, stood Zwernitz Castle, which Friedrich remodeled into a summer residence. It lacked only a *Lustgarten*, or a garden for pleasure and entertaining. The chosen architect, Joseph Saint-Pierre, provided for a diversity of wooden structures, which are all gone today, and an Oriental pavilion that one reached through a garden of parterres with boxwood and paths of colored gravel. All this activity brought to light an extraordinary natural curio that lay just behind the garden, one that Wilhelmine would transform into the most glorious "garden of rocks." Although cast aside for a long time, it recovered well from the period of neglect.

Opposite: Since 1774 visitors have entered the garden through this mysterious, vertical crack, which holds the promise of adventure.

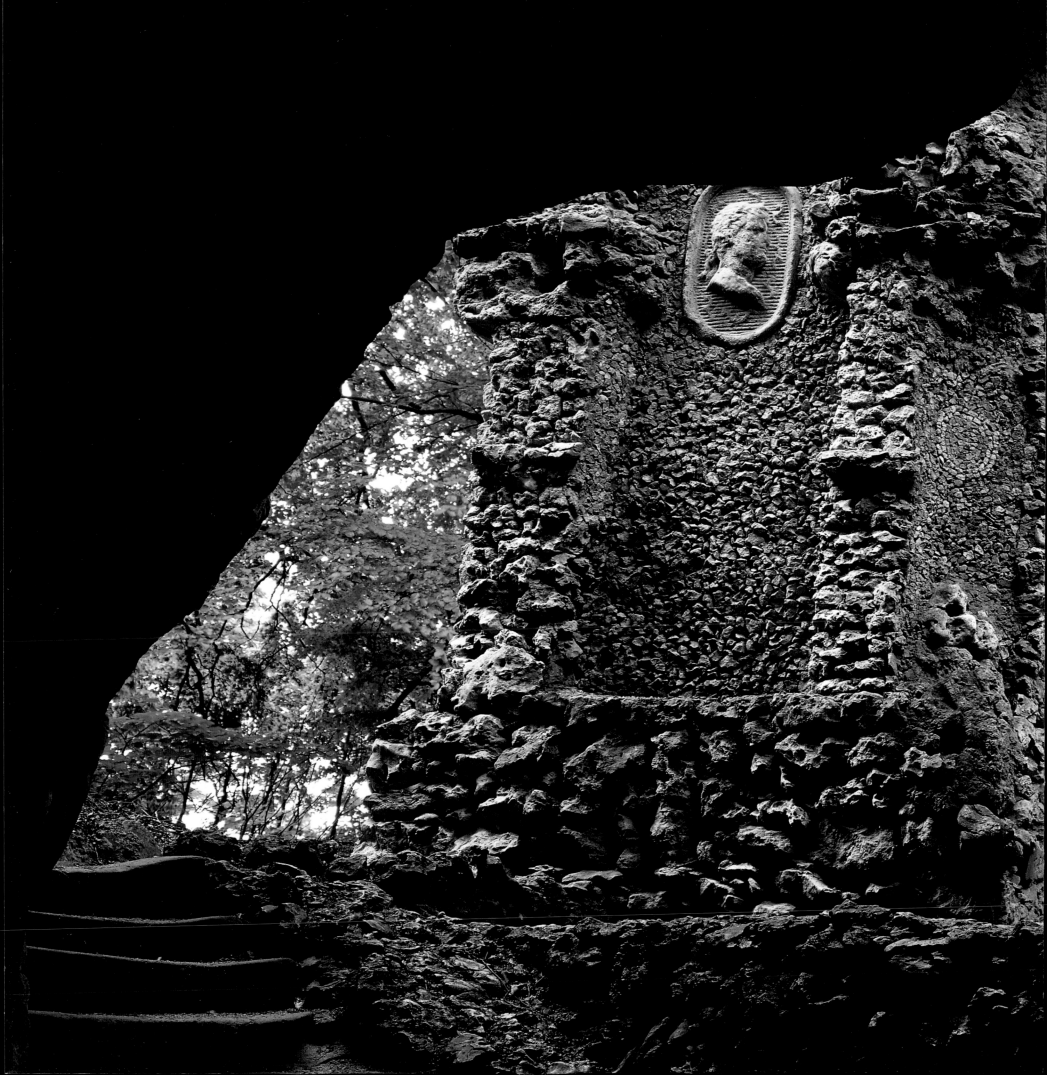

Panorama: The Theater of Stone, an
artificial ruin decorated with stones
and medallions worn with age

Above: A grotesque mask carved into
the pediment over the theater entrance

Through an odd fault between two boulders, one entered into a landscape of standing rocks, rock slides, crevices, outcroppings, and dark, mossy caves that provided refreshment in summer. The margrave imagined that this somewhat menacing place could serve as the setting for the *Adventures of Telemachus, Son of Ulysses*. It was a serial publication in eighteen sections by Fénelon, a French bishop, author, and Catholic apologist. Although he was the grandson of Louis IV, Fénelon was from a family of modest means. In the "garden of rocks," Wilhelmine saw the Isle of Ogygia, where the nymph Calypso cried over the departure of Ulysses but rejoiced at the arrival of his son, Telemachus. With simple installations— inscriptions, medallions, colored stone, rockeries, and even glass—she transformed this wild place into a poetic story. The walkway leads to surprise after surprise, until it reaches a theater of greenery with arches open to the trees. Before Romanticism and the German Sturm und Drang movement, Wilhelmine created a poetical universe that far surpassed the lovely Rococo style of the time. She also developed the first landscape garden in Germany, and Europe. Wilhelmine was a sensitive and well-informed woman. As the daughter and sister of the kings of Prussia and a cousin of the king of England, she received many illustrious visitors, including Voltaire, who wrote her eulogy ("O Bareith! O Virtue! O Graces adored!"). She was probably current with the latest trends in English gardens through her own correspondence or by reading the published accounts of travelers. Certain aspects of Sanspareil—the statuary and architectural sculptures—remind us of Italy and its extraordinary sculpture garden, Bosco Sacro di Bomarzo, even though it was nearly forgotten after 1740. About her dear Sanspareil, she wrote to her brother: "Nature herself was the architect."

This moss-covered stairway leads to a little belvedere above a grotto dedicated to Aeolus, god of the wind.

The Keukenhof

The Keukenhof is a relatively recent type of garden that is often called the "floral exhibition park." The democratization of European gardens since the beginning of the twentieth century and the enthusiasm of amateur gardeners who don't hesitate to travel hundreds of miles to purchase new plants explain the success of this formula, which the Dutch town of Lisse has brought to a peak.

Above: In the mist of early spring, the immense multicolored beds of tulips, grape hyacinths, and narcissi thrill visitors to the Keukenhof with their size and intensity.

Opposite: The grand effect of these plantings is produced by their density and the sheer numbers of flowers.

The Keukenhof, a Dutch word for kitchen garden, was originally established in the fifteenth century by a countess who was briefly married to a crown prince of France and wished her household to have fresh herbs and vegetables. After many ups and downs, the garden was turned into a park in 1840 by a fashionable father-and-son landscaping team named Zocher, who gave the estate a highly cultivated English look. In 1949, perhaps foreseeing the rise of Dutch horticulture, the mayor of the district where the Keukenhof is located, along with several bulb growers, decided to create a showcase of its potential glory. On seventy-nine acres, the Keukenhof today displays more than six million flowers grown from bulbs every year: tulips, of course, but also narcissi, crocuses, and daffodils. Most of the displays involve masses of huge flowers, which seem to enjoy the extravagance, with some of the tulips growing well over three feet in height. Here the smallest border extends for hundreds of feet, and a bed of daffodils is more like a carpet of many thousands of flowers. The overall impression is that of the fields of flowers stretching to infinity that one sees from the highway or from an airplane on the approach to Amsterdam.

Unlike summer gardens, the delirious splendor of Keukenhof attains its height in mid-April, when hundreds of thousands of flowers bloom in unison under the intent gaze of thousands of fascinated amateur gardeners.

The Keukenhof has transformed an English-style park into a massive carpet of bulbous flowers, which are maintained each day by thirty-five gardeners.

Tulips, hyacinths, narcissi, and fritillaria
bloom beneath a flowering apple tree.

The curving bank of a pond is
emphasized with a planting of narcissi.

Russia Peterhof

Peterhof, which means "Peter's Court," was completely ravaged in 1945. Located on the outskirts of St. Petersburg, the estate was bombarded, vandalized, and wrecked during one of the bloodiest sieges in history. Today, Peterhof has regained its gilded beauty, its splendid parks and dazzling fountains. The restoration of one of the largest and most magnificent palaces of the eighteenth century is a great symbol of Russia's cultural revival and of its new ties with Europe. That was exactly what Peter the Great had in mind when he decided to build it early in the eighteenth century.

Above: The rear facade of the palace of Peter the Great, seen from the Upper Gardens. The Fountain of Neptune is in the foreground.

Opposite: The wall at Marly Palace, planted with a row of lime trees shaped into spheres, protects the gardens from the wind.

The gardens of Peterhof are something of a travel memoir, for when Tsar Peter I visited Versailles in 1716, he came away fascinated. His interest in the gardens, however, was hardly new. In the city of St. Petersburg, which he founded in 1703, he had already created the Summer Garden, which he entrusted to Dutch gardeners who were greatly influenced by the French style. The tsar also had a country residence on the Gulf of Finland, the magnificent Strelna Palace, which is not far from where Peterhof was built. At Strelna, Peter enjoyed a park on two levels, a canal, and lovely fountains, but the limited amount of water prevented him from exploring further enhancements. The water fountains at Versailles, as well as the great canal and the views opening out on an infinite landscape, had enchanted him, and he wished to create something equally wonderful for his new summer palaces, Monplaisir and the Upper or Great Palace, on which he had begun construction in 1714, working with the architect Johann Friedrich Braunstein, a disciple of the prominent German sculptor and architect Andreas Schluter.

When he was in Paris, Peter had met an architect and student of the celebrated André Le Nôtre, Jean-Baptiste Le Blond (1679–1719), whom he commissioned to become chief architect of the project. Le Blond set to work immediately upon his arrival in Russia in September 1716. The work site was gigantic, and the project was made all the more difficult by the tsar's involvement in even the smallest details. Peter knew the Peterhof site very well, as he had often sojourned there with his wife, Catherine. Le Blond died suddenly in 1719, but his plans were taken up by an Italian architect, Niccolo Michetti, who was primarily responsible for the elaborate waterworks, made possible by the discovery in 1720 of abundant sources of water not far

The Golden Hill Cascade. At left is Marly Palace, which overlooks the Gulf of Finland.

These replacements conformed to the neoclassical style of the palace alterations made after 1745, so it is difficult to establish a precise theme in the decoration, as at Versailles, although the traditional iconography of the sea—Neptune, sirens, sea monsters, dolphins, nymphs, and so on—is well represented, along with the classical nudes of antiquity.

Peterhof celebrates water in its myriad beautiful forms. The gardens were built with 173 fountains (although this number is slightly smaller today), which are supplied by a canal twelve miles long. The pools in the Upper Garden are the reservoirs for the water sprays in the Lower Park. Aside from the Great Cascade, each part of the park is centered on an aquatic theme: the Adam and Eve Fountains, the Italian and French Fountains, and then the Cascades of the Golden Hill and the British Exchequer—this last guarded by strange polychrome dragons—and the Seashell Cascade in the Chinese Garden. There are also amusing surprise fountains, like the benches that startle anyone who sits on them, the umbrella fountain that sprays visitors standing under it, the tulip fountains that splash viewers, and the tree fountains whose branches contain water jets that create a pinwheel effect. Other water themes are more classical, such as the Fountain of Psyche, the Danaid Fountain, and the Sun Fountain, whose rays emit powerful jets of water.

Today Peterhof is one of the most popular tourist sites in Russia. Visitors marvel at the palace and its fountains and delight in its charming pavilions. Strolling in the impeccable gardens of the Marly Palace, with its trees carefully shaped in garlands around the water's edge, viewers imagine an idyllic eighteenth century in a country that has just been opened to the West. One would do well to remember Peter's true nature, however, as recalled by Wilhelmine, margrave of Bayreuth, in her description of a visit made by the Russians ("the Barbarian court") to her father, Friedrich Wilhelm I of Prussia. She describes Peter's frequent convulsions and his rude table manners; how he made the tsarina kiss a priapic statue with the threat "*Kop ab*" (It'll be your head); and his penchant for what we would call practical jokes (which may explain the surprise benches and the umbrella fountain at Peterhof). For the record, this "enlightened" autocrat was known for his cruelty, lack of respect for people, and disdain for all that was Russian. Peterhof, then, is a curious manifestation of a brutal prince's taste for refinement, which he appreciated for its symbolic value. Yet we cannot reduce this palace and its gardens to a development center for the Russian nobility, or dismiss it as a mere window onto the luxury enjoyed by European royalty of that era. If Peterhof had been only that, we could not admire it as we now do.

Panorama: The Grand Cascade literally springs from the base of the palace and descends into a vast pool holding a bronze statue of Samson holding open the mouth of the lion. This work was cast by Mikhaïl Kozlovsky in 1802 to replace the original lead sculpture made in 1736 to celebrate the victory of Peter the Great over Sweden.

from the work site. Peterhof would soon become one of the largest water gardens in the world.

Peter the Great built his Upper Palace on a butte overlooking the Gulf of Finland. In the distance twinkled the lights of St. Petersburg, the new capital, which lay beneath the watchful eyes of its ruler. This position allowed for the installation of two huge parks, the Upper Garden, which faces the land, and the Lower Park, which faces the sea, with the palace linking the two. The link is formed by fountains and a pool in front of the palace, whose overflowing waters create powerful waterfalls as they surge down two staircases of marble and gold and empty into a round, ornamental pool fifty-three feet below. The waters of the ornamental pool flow into a large canal that runs out to the Baltic Sea. The tsar often traveled by boat—the Russian roads, where there were any, were famous for their pitiful condition—and he liked the idea that in wintertime he could arrive directly at his residence by this method. The ornamental pool is one of the focal points of the entire composition. In its center is a stony island that serves as a base for a gilded sculptural scene symbolizing Russia's victory over Sweden in the Great Northern War (1700–1721). There a statue of a muscular Samson opens the jaws of a lion to release a jet of water sixty-six feet high. A host of gilded statues around the borders of the ornamental pool and at the edges of the marble waterfall peoples this grandiose spectacle.

The statuary of Peterhof has a rather complicated history. At first, commissions for the statues were given even before places had been found for them, and once they were installed, the salty air did its work on the stone and the bronze. Many were replaced at the end of the eighteenth and nineteenth centuries, and of course again after 1945.

With its innumerable fountains, Peterhof is the largest water garden in the world. Pictured here is the Sun Fountain with its sparkling water jets.

Huntington Botanical Gardens

UNITED STATES
• San Marino, CA

Humans have always wished to understand nature, and the knowledge of plants was essential in agricultural societies. Early on the United States became both an exporter of indigenous plants and an importer of species from Europe. In southern California at San Marino, the Huntington Botanical Gardens respond more to the passion of the enthusiast than to the researcher at a level their European counterparts only rarely attain.

Above: Garden within a garden, the Desert Garden possesses the most beautiful collection of cacti in the United States.

Opposite: A stunning collection of echinocactus, or hedgehog cactus, the largest of which grow to three feet in diameter and can retain up to fifty-three quarts of water

Henry Edwards Huntington (1850–1927) belonged to the generation of bold industrialists who made the United States the world's primary economic power. Son of a man who had a grocery and hardware business on the East Coast, Henry was the nephew of Collis P. Huntington, who had made his fortune in the California railroads and brought the young man into the business. Henry created the idea of a streetcar network in Los Angeles, which became an intercity line, which within a few years served hundreds of towns in southern California. In 1900 he was fifty years old, very wealthy, and also heir to his uncle's fortune. Like many great American businessmen, Henry decided to dedicate himself to a noble work that he could leave to posterity.

In 1902 he acquired the ranch of San Marino, then planted in citrus orchards and located on a beautiful site in the San Gabriel Valley in full view of the snow-covered peaks of the Sierra Madre Mountains. He wanted to create there a kind of cultural haven, and he needed a handsome building for his library, a gallery for the paintings he had collected over the course of twenty years, and gardens to frame them both. In 1914 he moved into his elegant Georgian house, now a museum, where one can admire his important collection of furniture and English portraits of the eighteenth century, of which *Blue Boy* by Thomas Gainsborough and *Pinkie* by Thomas Lawrence are the best known. Built in 1902, the research library houses the most important private collection of incunabula, or books published in the fifty years between the invention of the printing press (about 1450) and the year 1500.

The garden, however, represents an entirely different sort of adventure. Through happenstance Huntington met in 1904 a talented young gardener named William Hertrich (1904–1966), a man in whom he quickly

The North Vista is bordered by eighteenth-century statues that once decorated the gardens of a villa near Padua.

192

placed his trust and who would spend fifty years of his life building and developing the most beautiful gardens in California. The Huntington Botanical Gardens comprise several individual gardens organized by type or by climate spread over 150 acres. Sharing this space are the museum, the library, the Boone and Scott Galleries, a restaurant, and a huge parking lot.

The Rose Garden, planted in 1908, was one of the first gardens. It contains many old varieties, with some specimens from the Middle Ages and the Renaissance. This garden is one of the rare places where one can find most of the notable roses, especially English ones, developed from the 1920s to the present day. A little further on, the recent Shakespeare Garden contains only plants that are found in William Shakespeare's plays. One of the most spectacular creations at Huntington Gardens is the Desert Garden. With its 25,000 xerophytes (plants adapted to arid conditions), it is the most important collection in the world of plants from desert climates growing in the open air. One would be hard-pressed in the deserts of Arizona and Nevada to find plants of such great variety that are as rare and ancient or found in such amazing density. Newcomers to the garden include the ancient *Cereus xanthocarpus*, which weighs more than fifteen and a half tons; the *Welwitschia*, a living fossil that never produces more than two leaves, although each one is about ten feet long; and the scary "devil cactus" of Baja California, which grows to resemble a group of entwined snakes.

A great moor of four and a half acres is home to a thousand varieties of camellias, and beyond it lies the Japanese Garden, which was planned in 1911. It was planted in a small gorge, affording Huntington the opportunity to create ponds, stairways, and a moon bridge. In fact, the garden had been purchased in Pasadena, and the plants and the Japanese house were transported to San Marino in a convoy of twenty-five trucks. A recent addition is the Zen Garden, in which the raking of stones and a few rocks are made to resemble the ocean. A short distance away, the visitor can find an exceptional collection of bonsai, after which come the Australian Garden, the Subtropical Garden, and the Jungle Garden, where running streams flow into waterfalls. The gardens of the temperate zones are populated by statues, and most impressive are those from early-eighteenth-century Padua that stand in two rows along the great *allée*.

Huntington Botanical Gardens and its 14,000 plant species is one of the most visited tourist sites in southern California, and it has at its disposal a research center in botany that was established by its founder and by William Hertrich. This remarkable organization with its spectacular gardens inspires all visitors with an interest in plants and nature, which was one of Huntington's goals when he founded the gardens in 1919. He bequeathed his estate to the state of California.

The peristyle of the Virginia Steele Scott Gallery of American Art. In the foreground is part of the Shakespeare Garden, which is composed exclusively of plants mentioned in the dramatist's plays.

Following pages: The Japanese Garden, created in 1912, grows more than 2,000 varieties of camellias. The tea house in the background, from the Meiji period, was brought from Japan.

Magnolia Plantation

UNITED STATES
Charleston, SC •

The fame of the Magnolia Plantation is not the result of the recent popularity of the art of gardening. As early as 1900, the Baedeker Guide listed it among the three most important tourist sites in the United States, alongside the overwhelming but flattering company of Niagara Falls and the Grand Canyon. In fact, the plantation had been known for its gardens since the seventeenth century.

Above: On the bank of the Ashley River, a hundred-year-old Virginia holm oak is laden with Spanish moss, a plant that survives on the ambient light and humidity.

Opposite: This Victorian house, originally built in a neighboring town, was dismantled and rebuilt on the Magnolia Plantation after the Civil War.

When Ann Fox married Thomas Drayton, the son of a wealthy planter in Barbados, her dowry included a plantation in South Carolina, not far from Charleston. In the 1670s, the couple moved to the plantation and built a fine house surrounded by formal gardens. A labyrinth inspired by that at Hampton Court but planted in camellias and holly was a joy for its beauty as well as its scent. The crops prospered, and the garden flourished, but in 1800 the house burned to the ground. It was quickly replaced by another house, which General Sherman reduced to ashes during the Civil War. Rebuilt in a Victorian style, the plantation house today welcomes thousands of visitors. About 1830, a member of the family, the Reverend John Grimke Drayton (1815–1891), was directed by his doctors to get regular exercise; and this he did by creating gardens from what was once marshland.

This self-taught gardener had no doubt read some of the English works on parks and gardens written at the end of the eighteenth century. He endeavored to make the most of the natural setting and the land that surrounded him. The Carolinas are tough country, in which the charms of the South derive more from the will of the planters and the hard labor of slaves than from the natural conditions. But Reverend Drayton had the brilliant idea to install an unobtrusive and indigenous order over vast expanses of swamp and hostile forest. For the most part he chose plants that were native to the locale, such as the bald cypress, Virginia holm oaks, magnolias, azaleas—which originated there—and Cherokee roses, which scale the trunks of trees seeking sunshine.

There are two aspects of Magnolia Gardens that fascinate visitors: the blackness of the waters and the ubiquity of Spanish moss, which seems to link all the trees with natural swags. The black reflections in the ornamental lakes are caused by a tannic acid emitted from the roots of the bald cypress. They provide a mysterious and poetic foreground to the blooming magnolias, azaleas, and the young cypress leaves. As to the Spanish moss, it is *Tillandsia usneoides* (named for the Swiss naturalist Tilland and the word *usnéoïde*, which means "resembling a mousse"), a plant without roots that subsists on light and humidity and uses the trees merely as a natural support. A member of the Bromeliad family, Spanish moss, in its five hundred species, essentially developed in the tropics of the Western Hemisphere. The plants have long been harvested for use as fodder, insulating material, or a stuffing for mattresses. Their strange, somewhat unsettling appearance and pronounced scent, particularly in spring, have given rise to numerous legends.

Today the Magnolia Plantation and Gardens, on the National Register of Historic Places, offers spectacular enclosed Barbados tropical gardens that you can explore in a small boat as well as the eighteenth-century garden, the topiary garden, a labyrinth, and the Audubon Garden, a refuge of 128 acres for local wildlife and plant life.

Panorama: The trees and azaleas are reflected in the totally still water of Schoolhouse Pond.

The dogwood tree, *Cornus florida*, pictured against a background of *Azalea indica*, produces abundant blossoms on long, spindly branches that sway gracefully in the slightest breeze.

The Long White Bridge was built by
John Grimke Drayton in the
nineteenth century. In the foreground
are bald cypress trees.

Cypress Gardens

UNITED STATES
Moncks Corner, SC •

Exotic and strange is the untamed atmosphere of this immense water garden near Charleston, South Carolina. Planted on the site of former rice paddies, Cypress Gardens extends for nearly two hundred acres, much of which is occupied by a shallow lake, whose dark waters look like a mysterious mirror of unknown magic.

Above: White narcissi emerge from the marshes and still waters to cheer the somber landscape.

Opposite: The roots of the bald cypress are aquatic and develop growths called pneumatophores, which enable them to breathe underwater.

Until the Civil War, the plantation of Dean Hall put more than five hundred slaves to work in the rice paddies, which were watered by a natural lake. After the estate was abandoned, the new owners, the Kittredges, transformed it into a game reserve in 1927, and it was they who conceived the idea of planting azaleas in the marshlands. Azaleas imported from India and Japan, rhododendrons, and various types of hyacinth adapt very well to this subtropical climate, which is incredibly humid. The brilliant spectacle provided by their vibrant blooms is a unique experience, especially when it is seen mirrored in the lake.

The azaleas have grown dense enough to form copses and thickets, but they are still dominated by the thousands of majestic bald cypress trees, which managed to survive Hurricane Hugo in 1996, unlike other leafy trees, which virtually disappeared. Spanish moss hangs in festoons from branches of the cypress trees, whose trunks are adorned with purple wisteria. The only reminder of the past lies in the ruins of a Spanish-style chapel and a bridge with a railing covered in Cherokee roses, the mythic flower of that tribe of Native Americans. One can walk through the gardens, using the old dikes of the rice paddies as footpaths, or one may slide through in a flat-bottomed boat. It is not unusual for an alligator to fix an inscrutable gaze on visitors, or that a fearsome water snake will ruffle the surface of the waters. Every vision of paradise is unique.

As soon as the ground dries, azaleas, wisteria, and Cherokee roses reign over the trees and the thickets.

Suzhou

Located west of Shanghai, the ancient imperial residence of Suzhou contains more than two hundred gardens, of which more than sixty are in a good state of preservation. Four of these are part of UNESCO's list of World Heritage Sites: Garden of the Surging Waves (1044), Lion Grove Garden (1342), Garden of the Humble Administrator (1509), and Lingering Garden (1522).

In China the art of gardening was always one of the occupations of the intellectual, considered to be on the same level with literature and painting, for its emphasis on meditation in communion with nature. The first emperors attempted to make their parks in the image of the paradise of the Immortals to which they aspired, and this concept influenced gardeners until the end of the nineteenth century. Water, mountains (composed of rocks fashioned by nature), and the hut, or pavilion, for meditation played an essential role; vegetation, which came later, was associated with thoughts and emotions.

The Lion Grove Garden and the Garden of the Surging Waves, despite their reduced size (about four thousand square feet), encompass all the characteristic traits of the classical garden, of which architecture is an essential component. The gardens are isolated by a wall and are entered through a circular doorway, or moon door. Water is ever-present, but one must not be able to discern where it is going or from where it came. The most striking aspect of the garden is the way it is perceived by the visitor, to whom it is revealed scene by scene as one proceeds on a walkway alongside the buildings and within a covered gallery that allows one to stroll sheltered from the sun and rain. The windows, called *louchouang*, are cut into the walls of the gallery in the shapes of flowers, vases, or vegetal motifs. The garden is viewed like a painted scroll that is unrolled slowly, and indeed these natural settings evoke the subjects and themes of Chinese painting. Precious, refined, and clever, the gardens of China have fascinated travelers from the West since the time of Marco Polo.

The moon door, a typical element in classical Chinese architecture, leads to the Lion Grove Garden, which is named for the stones that are perched like lions at attention.

In the Garden of the Pavilion of
Waves, built in the twelfth century, a
gallery with windows of filigreed design
allows visitors to enjoy a view of the
garden even in the rain.

A marble window with an intricate
openwork design in the Garden of the
Surging Waves

The Garden of the Surging
Waves, created in 1044
during the Song dynasty, is
one of the most ancient in
Suzhou. A covered walkway
winds around an
ornamental lake.

Japan Gardens of the Kyoto Temples

As the capital of imperial Japan from 794 to 1868, Kyoto has no fewer than 1,650 Buddhist temples, 400 Shinto sanctuaries, and 100 notable gardens. Miraculously spared from the atomic bomb of 1945, this large city has tried valiantly to preserve the treasures of its long history and remains one of the principal repositories of Japanese religion and culture. As such, Kyoto is a living testament of the strength and tenacity of their ancient religious and philosophic beliefs. And the gardens are their poetic expression.

Above: Raking ceremony at Ryoanji (fifteenth century). The fifteen stones that enliven this carefully raked rectangle of pebbles cannot all be seen at one time.

Opposite: The dry garden at Nanzenji

Long influenced by China, the Japanese garden enjoyed its most creative period from the eighth to the sixteenth centuries. The great garden reference manual known as the *Sakuteiki*, from the second half of the eleventh century, laid out the fundamental rules for creating a garden where nature

is at its ease, where the desires of its elements—streams, islands, stones, and wood—are respected, where asymmetry with buildings is cultivated. Finally, the author provides guidance on bringing out the spirit of the place using one's personal taste and the natural elements.

These principles apply to the ancient Japanese garden of all types, but the temple garden served a special purpose other than relaxation and the enjoyment of the court or aristocratic families. The bit of nature contained within the temple was meant as an aid for the monks in their meditations. Thus the garden projected an image of the sacred essence of nature. The most brilliant practitioner of this art was the Zen master Muso Kokushi (1275–1351), who created the gardens of Saihoji and Tenryuji, which are famous for their moss-covered grounds, where one can see the tree roots underneath. Nevertheless, the dry garden,

Above: A couple meditating in front of the Jizoin garden

Opposite: Saihoji, or the Garden of Mosses, dates from the middle of the fourteenth century. The principle behind the cultivation of mosses at this historic monument was later used in numerous Japanese gardens.

At the edge of the pond of the Golden Pavilion, miniature pine trees are multiplied by their reflection in the water.

The Golden Pavilion, built in 1394 as a
retirement estate for a powerful shogun,
was later transformed into a temple.

called *karesanui*, is the perfect expression of this art. In ancient times, the Japanese arranged stones, sometimes of unusual shapes, and often surrounded them with sand or white pebbles to signal the presence of a divinity. During the great Heian period (794–1185), this practice nearly disappeared, and stones were treated as symbolic or figurative islands in the pond-gardens. However, the dry garden reappeared during the Kamakura period of the twelfth to fourteenth centuries and found favor among the monks of the Zen Buddhist temples.

Ryoanji, "temple of the peaceful dragon," the most famous stone garden in the world, now finds itself on the line where the city meets the forest. When it was created, about 1490, Ryoanji was a garden surrounded by countryside. It still forms a rectangular area of 400 square yards, partially bordered by a low earthen wall reinforced with tiles. It also features a veranda on which one can sit and contemplate the arrangement—in Japanese, to meditate and to sit have almost the same meaning. There is an area of pale gray sand with an arrangement of fifteen stones, which appear to have been formed by nature even though one of them bears the discrete signature of Kawamono.

Kawamono was a landscape artist, but his role here remains unknown. A circle of moss like a halo surrounds the stones, a feature that is more or less important depending on the season. The sand is very carefully raked, following the longest line of the area, and the rake also makes curved lines around each stone. Whatever the spectator's position, he can never see the fifteen stones together, only fourteen at most, and one of the stones always remains hidden. We can count at least fifteen theories on the meaning of this composition, from the tigress showing her cubs how to cross a river to the sea and its islands symbolizing the birth of Japan, or a representation of the void, or an explanation of numerological order. These theories generally neglect the fact that this garden has evolved since its creation. It has certainly been enlarged—its walls, which date only to the eighteenth century, have been modified; one used to be able to walk directly on the sand, for example. Moreover, the garden should not be evaluated from a drawing or be viewed from above; it was to have been seen from the superior's house, where one used to see an empty white rectangle in the foreground before gardens were visible above the low walls.

The theory of Günter Nitsche, the great interpreter of Japanese gardens, on the meaning of Ryoanji seems the most convincing. The stones were the medium of meditation, which redirected the incoming flow of energy of the object—the stone—toward the consciousness of the meditator. The consciousness comes back to its true self through the disappearance of the ego.

Panorama: The garden of the Temple of Tenryuji, designed by the great Zen priest, Muso Kokushi, is one of the largest Zen gardens in existence.

Imperial Gardens of Kyoto

Were the gardens of the Japanese destined to look just like those of the Chinese? Although Japanese civilization has been profoundly influenced by China since the sixth century, the extraordinary capacity of the Japanese to assimilate and appropriate the ideas of others made the concept of a garden an authentic Nipponese art.

From the eighth century on, descriptions of life at the Japanese imperial court often include settings in water gardens—bodies of water, often artificial ones, designed for walks and visual enjoyment, aquatic areas rather than gardens in the usual sense of the term. The elements of these ornamental lakes were clearly inspired by the Chinese, such as the islands that could be linked to the shore by bridges, the wooden piers leading to docks on which music pavilions were built, the arrangements of carefully selected stones meant to resemble mountains or islands, and the areas reserved for growing water lilies. In the eleventh century, the classic treatise on gardens, *Sakuteiki* (Records of Garden-Making) spoke of the sea, of waves and the shore, and of peninsulas. If most of such creations have disappeared, the archeological digs conducted in the ancient capital of Nara allow us to envisage a more precise picture of the original form. The residents of Kyoto still enjoy sailing in the autumn to view the moon on the *Osawanoike* (Big Marshy Pond) created for Emperor Saga (809–823).

The plant garden was developed during the Heian period, when no one would think of designing a beautiful residence, let alone a palace, without a garden. Here we find various ways to define the limits of outdoors, and of indoors, and these elements remain central to Japanese architecture even today. Typically, a planted area would be surrounded on three sides by the main building, the outbuildings, and the covered walkways leading to the pavilions. The garden featured either a stream or an ornamental lake, whose position was determined by geomancy (a precursor of feng shui). In the imperial palaces, the garden was separated from the main residence by an area of white sand, symbol of the emperor's divinity. Fenced gardens could be set up between the buildings, and these were planted in flowers of a similar variety and color, like early versions of the monochromatic Edwardian gardens.

Opposite: A walkway in the garden of the imperial palace of Kyoto Gosho, which was reserved for members of the court until the court was moved to Tokyo in 1868.

A visit to a Japanese garden requires the knowledge of certain codes or historical practices. For example, the classic imperial or aristocratic gardens of the twelfth to sixteenth centuries were composed of a series of scenes that had to be viewed from a precise spot to be appreciated. This was a far cry from the English parks of the eighteenth century with their changing perspectives. Although the symbolism was ever present and fundamental, it was only decipherable by one with a cultivated taste. The modern or uneducated visitor would likely pass by unaware of the desired effect, which might be the representation of a famous landscape, the symbol of a religious presence, an allusion to an ancient legend, or the life of Buddha.

Further on, the trimming of a tree according to the precepts of the art of *o-karikomi* might appear strange to the average visitor, but viewed from a precise angle, the act represents whitecaps on the sea. Miniaturization is practiced in two ways. Some gardens are miniature universes that reproduce a famous landscape or nature on a reduced scale; in other gardens, clipping and pruning are employed to keep the size of trees to a specific dimension in order to retain over the course of years the original harmony in appearance. Less visible in Kyoto, largely because today the modern city encircles the gardens, another element of the Japanese garden is the "borrowed view," which is practiced by landscapers who open up a view of a faraway mountain or of the sea in order to integrate them into their work.

The imperial gardens of Kyoto—Kyoto Gosho (Imperial Palace), Sento Gosho (Palace of the Retired Emperor), Kinkakuji (Golden Pavilion), and the imperial villa of Katsura (1620)—remain largely preserved testaments to an exceptional art. The meanings intended by their long-ago creators now elude Western eyes, as well as those of twenty-first-century Japanese. Nevertheless, in the presence of these harmonious colorations, the subtle refinements of the plantings and topiary, the exploitation of texture, and extreme sophistication in meaning, one can feel that these gardens were born of a deep religious respect and an infinite respect of nature.

Rebuilt in the nineteenth century, the garden of the Imperial Palace contains many decorative elements, such as exposed rocks and stone lanterns.

The gardens of Sento Gosho, the Palace of the Retired Emperor. An army of gardeners preserves the seventeenth-century appearance of the gardens.

The gardens of Sento Gosho were
created about 1630 for the emperor Go
Mizunoo. Many of the trees were
planted when the garden was first built,
including this massive pine tree
(opposite) and cherry tree (above).

National Orchid Garden

After a first attempt by Sir Stamford Raffles, founder of modern Singapore, an immense botanical garden of 128 acres was created on Government Hill in 1859. In 1995 it was enriched with the National Orchid Garden, a jewel that attracts 700,000 visitors each year.

Within seven and a half acres, this fascinating garden presents more than sixty thousand orchid plants of four hundred species, and more than two thousand hybrids, all in an "orchid house" created in situ. Curiously, the plants are arranged according to their seasonal preference, although this part of the world does not experience the change of seasons. The springtime zone is signaled with bright colors such as gold, yellow, and cream; the summertime zone is brightened with deep reds and roses; autumn is denoted by pastels, and winter with white and icy blue. The harmonies are enhanced by the skillful selection of trees and bushes, and complemented by various tropical plants sprinkled about the garden. A VIP (Very Important Plants) garden showcases rare orchids or those named after visiting celebrities, such as *Dendrobium* "Margaret Thatcher." Also found here is a local celebrity, the "Miss Joaquim Vanda" orchid, which appeared in the garden of one Miss Joaquim in 1983. A natural hybrid of *Vanda hookeriana* and *Vanda teres*, the orchid has generated a brisk business following research conducted at the Singapore Botanic Gardens, and was elected the national flower of Singapore in 1991.

Not far from Burkhill Hall, the former residence of the director of the Botanic Gardens, a border is planted in a *Vanda* hybrid.

The garden opened in 1955 and contains more than 60,000 orchids belonging to 400 species. Pictured here is a *Dendrobium sakura pink*.

Ayrlies

Auckland

NEW ZEALAND

Although New Zealand does not have an ancient horticultural tradition, the colonists brought their own with them—that of the English park and garden. During the 1960s, New Zealand farmers were not interested in any projects that removed land from cultivation, but Beverley McConnell was not discouraged. Her Ayrlies Gardens are among the most beautiful in the Southern Hemisphere and also one of the most visited tourist sites in Auckland.

Above: View toward the cypress pond and the summer kiosk. In the foreground, the perfectly acclimated arum plants thrive on New Zealand's North Island.

Opposite: A tiny waterfall at the foot of a tree fern

Beverley McConnell was the daughter of a doctor who passed on to her his love of nature, flowers, and gardening. She lived in Auckland and tended not only to her five children, but also to a small garden next to her house. She and her husband, Malcolm, desired a more agreeable life in the country, where they could plant trees in groups of different species, and interesting plants, and in 1967 they acquired a relatively vast tract of farmland in a hilly countryside a few miles from the capital, bordering the Gulf of Hauraki. Although the site was arable, it had virtually no plantings, since it had been a working farm. Malcolm gave four acres to his wife, who launched herself on a great adventure, the implications of which she never anticipated. At first she was inspired by the natural lay of the land and by the type of soil, which dictated to some extent the choice of plants. Then, during a trip to England, the couple visited Hampton Court, the palace of Henry VIII situated on the Thames. There Malcolm had a revelation about what the element of water could bring to their project. As soon as he returned home, he had four ponds dug, all connected by a pumping system to aerate the water and create waterfalls. Their tranquil garden took on a whole new dimension, and the country gardeners became landscape designers.

Forty years later, the trees and plants have matured; the water elements are integrated with the land as though nature had formed them; the gardens have found their balance; and Beverley has found a new reason to continue on, despite her husband's death in 1995. Although this accomplishment has been recognized by professionals all over the world, Ayrlies remains a private garden and retains a sense of the familial and the rural. Beverley employs four gardeners, and she stresses that this is a team effort. Oliver Briers built the pergolas himself and carved the benches into the mossy trunks of trees; he positioned the rocks to form the waterfalls and built the bridges. Neil Ross arrived more recently from England, flush with the prestige of having spent four years at the Sissinghurst Castle Gardens. The atmosphere here at Ayrlies is of a place that is loved, cared for, and lived in by its creator, and not of gardens that are maintained by talented employees.

The density of the plantings creates an illusion of luxuriance, with intense greens brightened by lupines and with crosiers of giant ferns or winding clematis vines, but the climate is not as serene here as one might suppose. The annual rainfall is quite high—more than 47 inches a year—and the clay soil is inhospitable to plants that prefer chalky or well-drained earth. A hard frost is rare, but the coast of Auckland is subject to drought, violent winds, and rainstorms. When a tornado recently uprooted six trees that were planted in the 1970s, it was necessary to replant the trees in groups so they could protect one another by serving as a windbreak. The principal species in these gardens are *Liquidamber styraciflua* (American sweetgum), *Taxodium distichum* (bald

Panorama: The large waterfall at the cypress pond, installed by Malcolm and Beverley McConnell in the late 1970s

cypress), and *Quercus palustris* (pin oak), all of which are happy in the undrained soil. There are also palm trees, aloe plants, fig and hazelnut trees, tea plants, shrubs, and bulbs from South Africa. Local species are still the most numerous, in particular conifers that are resistant to the wild turns in the weather, unlike imported plants that grow too quickly and then collapse. Flowers and flowering shrubs are perfectly adapted, as well as beautifully shaped cannas, dahlias, crocosmia, arum plants (such as the calla lily), and old roses. In fact, the species of the Northern and Southern Hemispheres combine to form a continual round of flowering throughout the year.

The four acres the McConnells began with grew to five and then to the twelve of today's gardens, which are surrounded by sixty-two acres of woodland. The process of landscaping nearly fifty acres of wetland has now linked the gardens to the ocean. When Beverley thinks back on all the effort expended, she is still amazed to have surpassed her dream of a "big garden." Her philosophy is simple but practical: Respect the land while integrating naturally into the site, and let the land dictate the quantities, the view, and, of course, the plantings. "Too many people settle in the country and proceed to ruin the very thing for which they came. They put up fences, plant trees in a straight line. . . . " There are no straight lines at Ayrlies; the visitor follows the twists and turns of winding paths or simply walks through the grass. The expanse of the ocean and the surrounding countryside, the varying gradations of the terrain, and the height of the trees combine to create a stunning sense of depth and beauty. The complexity of Ayrlies is proof that one's passion is generally well rewarded by nature.

Immense *Eucalyptus saligna, Cupressus sempervirens Swanes Gold,* and *Syagrus romanzoffiana* and giant tree ferns (*Cyathea medularis*) thrive in the humid conditions at Ayrlies Park.

Titoki Point Garden

Located in North Island, New Zealand, not far from Napier, the Titoki Point Garden are quite young, even though the robust trees and the tree ferns make us feel as though we have entered a primeval forest. One of its distinguishing characteristics is that it is the creation not of a wealthy aesthete with time on his hands but of a young, energetic farmer who attended a school of horticulture and fell in love with the art of gardening.

Gordon Collier, the creator of Titoki Point, was born in this extraordinary region, which was once covered with forests. Such was the density of these forests that they formed a veritable jungle, composed primarily of trees of the genus *Podocarpus*, such as totara, jakikatea, rimu, and titoki, after which the garden is named. The Collier family began clearing the land in 1927 and over the course of decades sowed vast lawns around the house; they planted classic and English roses by the hundreds, as well as pine trees and sequoias. Collier was not an enthusiast of this sort of artificial nature, and in 1965, when his parents entrusted him with half the property, he decided to realize his vision of an authentic New Zealand garden. More than forty years later, his objective has largely been realized. Not only is the new landscape reserved entirely for native species, but a nursery also allows the cultivation and sale of these plants and their seeds to many other countries.

Most successful gardens carefully conceal the efforts—often titanic—of their creators. Such is the case at Titoki Point, where Collier and his wife, Annette, have contended with the rolling land that requires the digging of a series of ponds, along with a great deal of terracing and the construction of steps to facilitate maintenance and to create the promenade. Moreover, the soil was composed mainly of clay, a substance quickly rendered into sticky paste by the typically abundant rainfall, and affected by droughts and sudden frosts. They composed stepped terraces between brilliant mixed borders, innumerable varieties of ferns, sumptuous thickets of rhododendron, and deciduous trees planted against a background of giant conifers. Titoki Point is a natural garden that adds to a new tradition of landscaping in these faraway islands that is influenced by the art of British life of which gardening is an essential component.

Created in the 1960s, Titoki is a paradise for botanists. In the foreground, large-leafed ligularias blend in beautifully with the yellow, bell-shaped flowers of *Primula helodoxa*, yellow iris, and ferns.

In the foreground, the base of a Japanese maple (*Acer palmatum dissectum*), blue hostas, and iris

Stunning ostrich fern, *Matteuccia struthiopteris*, and hostas against a background of *Dicksonia fibrosa* tree ferns

The humid climate encourages
the dense plant growth.
Behind the Snowden hostas
are *Primula candelabra* and, in
the background, the tree fern
Dicksonia fibrosa.

251

Bibliography

Acton, Harold. *The Villas of Tuscany*. Rev. ed. London: Thames & Hudson, 1987.

Adams, William Howard. *The French Garden, 1500–1800*. New York: Braziller, 1979.

Aslet, Clive. *The Last Country Houses*. New Haven/London: Yale University Press, 1982.

Bergé, Pierre. *Majorelle: A Moroccan Oasis*. New York: Vendome Press, 1999.

Brown, Jane. *Sissinghurst: Portrait of a Garden*. New York: Harry N. Abrams, 1990.
———. *Vita's Other World, a Gardening Biography of V. Sackville-West*. New York: Viking Penguin, 1987.

Clifford, Derek. *A History of Garden Design*. New York: Frederick C. Praeger, 1963.

Cooper, Guy, and Gordon Taylor. *Gardens for the Future: Gestures Against the Wild*. New York: Monacelli Press, 2000.

Cooper, Paul. *Gardens Without Boundaries*. London: Mitchell Beazley, 2003.

De Medici, Lorenza. *The Renaissance of Italian Gardens*. London: Chrysalis, 1990.

Girardin, René-Louis de. *Essay on Landscape: A Tour to Ermenonville*. New York: Garland Science, 1982.

Hadfield, Miles, Robert Harding, and Leonie Highton. *British Gardeners*. London: Zwemmer, Condé Nast, 1980.

Hertrich, William. *The Huntington Botanical Gardens, 1905–1949: Personal Recollections of William Hertrich*. Huntington, Calif.: Huntington Library, 1988.

Hobhouse, Penelope. *Gardens of Persia*. Carlsbad, Calif.: Kales Press, 2004.
———. *The Story of Gardening*. London: Dorling Kindersley, 2002.
———. *Gardening Through the Ages: An Illustrated History of Plants and Their Influence on Garden Styles—From Ancient Egypt to the Present*. New York: Simon and Schuster, 1993.

Houk, Walter. *The Botanical Gardens at the Huntington*. New York: Harry N. Abrams, 1996.

Hunt, John Dixon. *Italian Gardens: Art, Design, and Culture*. Cambridge: Cambridge University Press, 1996.
———. *The Genius of the Place: The English Landscape Garden, 1620–1800*. Cambridge, Mass.: MIT Press, 1988.

Hyams, Edward. *A History of Gardens and Gardening*. London: Orion, 1971.

Laird, Mark. *The Formal Garden: Traditions of Art and Nature*. London: Thames & Hudson, 1992.

Lord, Tony. *Planting Scenes from Sissinghurst*. London: National Trust, 2003.

Margrave de Bayreuth. *Mémoires de la Margrave de Bayreuth*. Paris: Mercure de France, 1967.

Mosser, Monique, and George Teyssot. *History of Garden Design: The Western Tradition from the Renaissance to the Present Day*. London: Thames & Hudson, 2000.

Nitschke, Günter. *Japanese Gardens*. New York: Taschen, 2002.

Nourry, Louis-Michel. *Les Jardins de Villandry: La nature mise en ordre*. Paris: Belin-Herscher, 2002.

Ohashi, Haruzo. *Japanese Garden Design*. Rutland, Vt.: Charles E. Tuttle, 1997.

Orsenna, Erik. *André Le Nôtre: Gardener to the Sun King*. New York: Braziller, 2001.

Otis, Denise. *Gardens for Pleasure: Four Centuries of the American Garden*. New York: Harry N. Abrams, 2002.

Ottewill, David. *The Edwardian Garden*. New Haven/London: Yale University Press, 1989.

Pereire, Anita. *Gardens for the 21st Century*. London: Aurum Press, 2000.
———. *Gardens of France*. New York: Harmony Books, 1983.

Ridley, Jane. *Edward Lutyens, His Life, His Wife, His Work*. London: Pimlico, 2003.

Rogers, Elizabeth Barlow. *Landscape Design: A Cultural and Architectural History*. New York: Harry N. Abrams, 2001.

Russell, Vivian. *Edith Wharton's Italian Gardens*. Boston: Bulfinch Press, 1998.

Saule, Beatrix. *Versailles Gardens*. New York: Vendome Press, 2002.

Sheeler, Jesse. *Little Sparta: The Garden of Ian Hamilton Finlay*. London: Frances Lincoln, 2003.

Steenberger, Clemens, and Reh Wouter. *Architecture and Landscape, The Design Experiment of the Great European Gardens and Landscapes*. Munich: Prestel-Verlag, 1996.

Strong, Roy C. *The Renaissance Garden in England*. London: Thames & Hudson, 1998.

Tun-Chen Liu. *Chinese Classical Gardens of Suzhou*. New York: McGraw-Hill, 1993.

de Virieu, Claire. *Apremont: A French Folly*. New York: Vendome Press, 1999.

Wharton, Edith. *Italian Villas and Their Gardens*. Los Angeles: Da Capo Press, 1977.

Wildenstein, Daniel. *Monet's Years at Giverny*. Reprint, New York: Harry N. Abrams, 1995.

Wilson, Andrew. *Influential Gardeners: The Designers Who Shaped 20th-Century Garden Style*. New York: Clarkson Potter, 2003.

Woodbridge, Kenneth. *Landscape and Antiquity: Aspects of English Culture at Stourhead, 1718 to 1838*. London: Clarendon Press, 1970.

Garden Information

BELGIUM

Château de Freÿr
Domaine de Freÿr ASBL
B-5540 Hastière
TEL. 011 32 (0) 82 22 22 00
www.freyr.be

CHINA

Classical Gardens of Suzhou
Suzhou Municipal Administrative,
Bureau of Gardens
Gongyuan Road 12
Suzhou
Jiangsu
TEL. 011 86 (512) 5224929
www.szgarden.com.cn

FRANCE

Le Bois des Moutiers
Route de l'Église
76119 Varengeville-sur-Mer
TEL. 011 33 (0)2 35 85 10 02

Château d'Ambleville
1 rue de la Mairie
95710 Ambleville
TEL: 011 33 (0)1 34 67 98 45
www.ambleville.com

Château de Courances
91490 Courances
TEL. 011 33 (0)1 64 98 41 18 OR
011 33 (0)1 40 62 07 62
EMAIL: clombardi@quilweb.com

Château de Villandry
37510 Villandry
TEL. 011 33 (0)2 47 50 02 09
www.chateauvillandry.com

Château de la Gaude
Les Pinchinats
13100 Aix-en-Provence
TEL. 011 33 (0)4 42 21 64 19
EMAIL: chateau-de-la-gaude@wanadoo.fr

Établissement public du musée et du domaine national de Versailles
Pavillon Dufour
RP 834
78008 Versailles cedex
TEL. 011 33 (0)1 30 83 78 00
www.chateauversailles.fr

Giverny
Fondation Claude Monet
84 rue Claude Monet
27620 Giverny
TEL. 011 33 (0)2 32 51 28 21
www.fondation-monet.com

Jardins d'Angélique
Manoir de Montmain
Hameau du Pigrard
76520 Montmain
TEL. 011 33 (0)2 35 79 08 12 OR
011 33 (0)6 25 84 41 53

Le Potager du Roi
École nationale supérieure du paysage
10 rue du Maréchal Joffre
78000 Versailles
TEL. 011 33 (0)1 39 24 62 82
www.potager-du-roi.fr

Parc floral d'Apremont-sur-Allier
Société hôtelière d'Apremont
18150 Apremont-sur-Allier
TEL. 011 33 (0)2 48 77 55 00
www.apremont-sur-allier.com

GERMANY

Schwetzingen Palace
Schloss Mittelbau
D-68723 Schwetzingen
TEL. 011 49 (0) 6202 81482
www.schloss-schwetzingen.de

Sanspareil
Felsengarten Sanspareil mit Morgenländischem Bau (Sanspareil Rock Garden and Oriental Building)
Schloss- und Gartenverwaltung Bayreuth-Eremitage
Haus Nr. 29
D-96197 Wonsees
TEL. 011 49 (0) 92 74 3 30 OR
011 49 (0) 92 74 12 21
www.schloesser.bayern.de

IRAN

Bagh-e Fin
Amirkabir Avenue
Kashan

Bagh-e Shahzdeh
Mahan

ITALY

Castello Ruspoli
Piazza della Repubblica, 9

01039 Vignanello (VT)
TEL. 011 39 0761 754 707 OR
011 39 0761 755 338
EMAIL: castelloruspoli@libero.it

Parco dei mostri, Bosco Sacro di Bomarzo
Loc. Giardino SNC
Bomarzo (Viterbo)
TEL. 011 39 0761 924029

Villa Visconti Borromeo Litta
Largo Vittorio Veneto, 8
20020 Lainate (Milano)
TEL. 011 39 02 93598266
www.comune.lainate.mi.it
www.amicivillalitta.it

Villa Gamberaia
Via del Rossellino, 72
50135 Settignano (Firenze)
TEL. 011 39 055 697205 OR 011 39 055 697090
www.villagamberaia.com

Villa Lante
Via Jacopi Barozzi, 71
01031 Bagnaia
TEL. 011 39 0761 288 008

JAPAN

www.joho-kyoto.or.jp/~english/Welcome.html
www.jnto.go.jp

MOROCCO

Majorelle Garden
Avenue Yacoub el Mansour
Marrakech
TEL. 011 212 044 30 18 52
www.jardin-majorelle.com

THE NETHERLANDS

The Keukenhof
Stationweg 166A
2161 AM Lisse
TEL. 011 31 (0) 252 465 555
www.keukenhof.com

NEW ZEALAND

Ayrlies
125 Potts Road
Whitford
Auckland
TEL. 011 64 9 530 8706 OR
011 64 9 530 8551

Titoki Point Garden
Koukoupo Road
RD 1
Taihape
TEL. 011 64 06 388 0085
EMAIL: titokipointgarden@xtra.co.nz

RUSSIA

The Peterhof State Museum-Reserve
ul.Razvodnaya, 2
198516 St. Petersburg
TEL. 011 7 812 427 7425
www.peterhof.org

SINGAPORE

Singapore Botanic Gardens and National Orchid Garden
1 Cluny Road
Singapore 259569
TEL. 011 65 6471 7361
www.nparks.gov.sg

UNITED KINGDOM

Levens Hall
Kendal
Cumbria
LA8 0PD
TEL. 011 44 (0) 1 5395 60321
www.levenshall.co.uk

Little Sparta
Ian Hamilton Finlay
Stony Path
Dunsyre
Lanark
ML11 8NG

Portrack House
Garden of Cosmic Speculation
Scotland
www.charlesjencks.com

Sissinghurst Castle Gardens
nr Cranbrook
Kent
TN17 2AB
TEL. 011 44 (0) 1 580 710700
www.nationaltrust.org.uk

Stourhead
Stourhead Estate Office
Stourton
Warminster
Wiltshire
BA12 6QD
TEL. 011 44 (0) 1 747 841152
www.nationaltrust.org.uk

UNITED STATES

Cypress Gardens
3030 Cypress Gardens Road
Moncks Corner, SC 29461
TEL. (843) 553-0515
www.cypressgardens.org

Huntington Botanical Gardens
The Huntington Library, Art Collections, and Botanical Gardens
1151 Oxford Road
San Marino, CA 91108
TEL. (626) 405-2100
www.huntington.org

Magnolia Plantation and Its Gardens
3550 Ashley River Road
Charleston, SC 29414
TEL. (843) 571-1266
www.magnoliaplantation.com

Photographing the Gardens

My work for this book covered most kinds of gardens, although I emphasized artistic expression through those places where "the plant appeared to serve the garden more than the garden served the plant." My research took three years and covered sixteen countries and states. During that time I lived a life of unheard-of privilege, that of traveling around the world to visit forty or so of the world's great gardens, places of my choosing, where I stayed for a while or returned to several times. Public or private, famous or unknown, all can be counted as superb examples of their type.

These were the places where, sometimes after long negotiations, I could work at my ease—that is, with complete freedom—very early and very late in the day; with the trust and lively interest of the gardens' authorities. These conditions were often ideal, as I felt I was at home, free to come and go as I pleased. I was sometimes the first to arrive and the last to leave, working from the first rays of dawn and picking up the task after the midday meal.

I have concentrated on the architectural aspect of the gardens, for which the panoramic format is very well suited. Each picture was inspired by my desire to convey an entire scene accurately, expressing its harmony of form, color, and light, rather than exploring a specific botanical interest.

It is rather unsettling to find that the task of photographing a garden, wherever in the world it might be, always makes the same demands. First, one must become as intimately acquainted with the place as possible, with its paths, its views, and the course of the sun—at what hours it will flood the scene with warmth or show certain forms in stark relief; how it affects a perspective when it shares the sky with light clouds or disappears in fog and mist. The quality of each shot results from conditions discovered as I went along. For some subjects, I had the maddening feeling that it would have been better if I had been there the previous evening, or if I had taken advantage of a mediocre forecast to survey the grounds in complete peace, without a camera, in order to avoid those inevitable first pictures that are often failures.

But soon, after I had traipsed back and forth across the land in every direction, morning and evening, it was possible to schedule the shots of each view within the most favorable hour and weather, realizing that sometimes one must return to reshoot—a yard closer, or tomorrow morning, or fifteen minutes earlier in the day, or worse, next year, but this time a week earlier. And a photographer has to know how to wait, and wait some more, and then work very quickly, for at these extreme hours the optimal conditions for the photograph do not linger for more than a quarter of an hour. Working at such speed, one must exercise care to avoid those fatal traces of footprints in the rose garden, or those crunching noises in the gravel paths that disturb a sleeping garden or startle a doe (as at Apremont) or a fox, whose presence is betrayed by his breath in the cold air (at Bois des Moutiers).

Each year the planting of a garden takes place over a period of several days. After that, nothing of note takes place other than the blooming of the flowers and the appearance of the sun and the clouds. It is these last two that guide my shots and permit me to capture the different moods with which they fill every place.

The pictures I present here, then, are a behind-the-scenes look at each garden, taken at those rare moments when the garden is open to no one.

The end of this voyage, I hope, will leave the reader wondering just what it is that makes a garden. I would hope that this book will make the reader want to visit these gardens, and, who knows, perhaps design one.

—Alain Le Toquin

I Remember...

— the very lively Azadeh, the Iranian lady draped in her black chador, who confided in me her pride that a man had come from so far away to take pictures of her garden at Bagh-e Fin.

— the delight of Ian Hamilton Finlay in making me hunt for the Tortoise-Tank in his garden at Little Sparta.

— Nigel Nicholson for giving me the honor of showing me his parents' garden at Sissinghurst

— the joyful face of Chris, the chief gardener at Levens Hall, who brought into the garden for me a stemmed glass with good French wine, while I took advantage of the last few minutes of the last moments of magnificent light on the topiaries.

— Lisa, responsible for public relations at Huntington, who was perturbed to learn that there was a problem with the Desert Garden.

— Kathy at Cypress Gardens for sending me a fax after we had left South Carolina saying, "The rhododendrons are blooming. . .come quickly."

— the old caretaker of Bagh-e Shahzdeh coming to open the garden gate at dawn and grumbling to my guide, Davoud, and to me.

— my mischievous guide in Japan, Kunio Kadowaki, who explained to me that after a photographer concentrates very hard, photographs end up hating their subject. (Clearly, I had not worked hard enough on them!)

— my "participation" in the Buddhist office, an obligatory first step before visiting the Garden of Mosses of Saihoji in Kyoto.

— Claudia, who showed me the sublime parterre on the first level of Castello Ruspoli and explained how the initials of her ancestors were carved into the boxwoods.

— Bev, who was so disappointed that she could not show me the Southern Cross in the sky on a slightly cloudy night in her garden of Ayrlies.

Acknowledgments

I thank all who opened the gates of their gardens to me and who facilitated the groundwork of this great undertaking:

The United States Embassy, Paris (Valérie Ferrière); the Italian Embassy, Paris (Géraldine Stefanon); the Japanese Embassy, Paris (Jun Fujiwara); Ambleville (Olivier Coutau-Bégarie); Apremont-sur-Allier (Elvire de Brissac); Ayrlies (Beverley McConnell); Bosco Sacro di Bomarzo (Giovanni Bettini); Castello Ruspoli (Claudia Ruspoli, Santino); Courances (Philippine de Ganay); Cypress Gardens (Kathy Woolsey); Freÿr (Axel Bonaert); Giverny (Claudette Lindsey); Huntington Botanical Gardens (Lisa Blackburn); Iran (Azadeh, Davoud Deghghan); The Keukenhof (Anne-Marie M.M. Gerards-Adriaansens); Kyoto (Kunio Kadowaki); La Gaude (Anne Beaufour); Le Bois des Moutiers (Antoine Bouchayer-Mallet); Les Jardins d'Angélique (Gloria and Yves Lebellegard); Levens Hall (Hal Bagot, Lydia and Chris Crowder); Little Sparta (Ian Hamilton Finlay, Pia Maria Simig); Magnolia Plantation (Taylor Drayton Nelson, Jane T. Willis); Majorelle (Pierre Bergé, Abderrazzak Benchâabane); Nymphaeum in Lainate (Marco Casara); Peterhof (Vadim Znamenov, Igor Guerassimov); Portrack House (Charles Jencks); Sanspareil (Mr. Schwarzott, Renate Gerspitzer); Schwetzingen (Harry Filsinger); Singapore (Abdul Hamid Hassan); Sissinghurst Castle (the National Trust, Nigel Nicolson, Sarah Cook); Stourhead (the National Trust, Katharine Boyd); Titoki Point Garden (Gordon Collier, Grant Pawson, Cynthia and Henry Collier); Versailles (Jeanne Latrobe, Sarah Simon); Villa Gamberaia (Luigi Zalum); Villa Lante (Rafaella Stratti); and Villandry (Henri Carvallo).

I also wish to express my appreciation to those who contributed their ideas and their talents to bring this project to publication. First, the wonderworkers Carole Daprey and Mathilde Delattre, who spent so many hours working on manuscripts and printers' proofs in the course of production. And without the thoughtful, well-crafted text of Michel Baridon and Jacques Bosser, this work would have been incomplete.

A bow of thanks, too, to Laure Buhart, Nathalie Lourau, and Patrick Marescaux, who were there from the beginning, when they commissioned several pieces of photo research. I am also grateful to Bernard Crespin and his team at the photography laboratory of Philab for their fine professionalism and to Cécile Vandenbroucque for her eye for detail during the production of the book.

I offer a special expression of thanks to Robert Fiess, who, when he was editor in chief of *Géo* magazine a long time ago, set me on the road to *The Most Beautiful Gardens in the World*.

A final thank-you to Michel Buntz, faithful road companion, who has been solicitous since I first entered this business, and to Hervé de La Martinière, both of whom were convinced of the value of this work.

Project Manager, English-language edition: Susan Richmond
Editor, English-language edition: Barbara Burn
Jacket design, English-language edition: Michael Walsh
Design Coordinator, English-language edition: Makiko Ushiba
Production Coordinator, English-language edition: Kaija Markoe

Maps by Evelyne Boyard

Library of Congress Cataloging-in-Publication Data

Le Toquin, Alain.
  [Jardins du monde. English]
  The most beautiful gardens in the world / introduction by Michel Baridon ; text by Jacques Bosser ; translated from the French by Clare Palmieri.
     p. cm.
  Includes bibliographical references and index.
  ISBN 0-8109-5584-9 (hardcover)
  1. Gardens. I. Bosser, Jacques. II. Title.

  SB465.L42 2004
  712--DC22

                        2004007441

Printed and bound in Italy
10 9 8 7 6 5 4 3 2 1

Harry N. Abrams, Inc.
100 Fifth Avenue
New York, N.Y. 10011
www.abramsbooks.com

Abrams is a subsidiary of